Jesse James and Lost Treasures of the Knights of The Golden Circle

Was He a Member and Did He Hide Some of Their Treasures. Was He Really Killed by Bob Ford, or Did He Live To Be 104 Years old.

By Noted Historian and Treasure Hunter

Dr. Roy William Roush, Ph.D.

Published by Front Line Press
Copyright February 2010
ISBN: 0-9723072-3-0
First Edition
Proudly Printed in The United States of America

This is my fourth book regarding the Knights of The Golden Circle and their activities. The others are: *The Mysterious and Secret Order of the Knights of The Golden Circle, How To Find The Treasures of The Knights of The Golden Circle,* and *Knights of The Golden Circle Treasure Signs.*

Copies of this or the other books can be ordered from Front Line Press
5150 Escobedo, Woodland Hills, CA 91364 (818) 888-5416
Or from the Website: KnightsofTheGoldenCircle.net

All rights reserved. No part of this book may be used, reproduced, photocopied, stored in any retrieval system, recorded, or transmitted by any means whatsoever without written permission from the author or publisher (except for brief quotes, reviews, references, or excerpts, provided proper credit is given.) Note- Some photos from the collection of James Dobson.

Dedication

This book is dedicated to all treasure hunters who are searching for that big treasure that they know is out there, someplace. Joe Hunter, after years of searching, finally succeeded in finding one of the big treasures that Jesse James and his gang had buried in the hills of Oklahoma--but they left more around that has not been found yet. The Knights of The Golden Circle also has left a lot of buried treasures around the country, Some of it has been found, but there is still more left to be discovered. None of these treasures are easy to find, so keep looking, think positively, and don't give up. Hopefully, the information in this book will help you find it. Good Luck!

Dr. Roy W. Roush

Other Credits of Dr. Roy William Roush

Author of the prize-winning book: Open Fire, a well-illustrated, 707-page story of the author's personal, front-line, combat experience with the 2nd Marine Division during the four epic battles of Guadalcanal, Tarawa, Saipan and Tinian in the South Pacific during World War II against the Japanese; plus four years as an Air Force Jet Fighter Pilot during the Korean War. The book was awarded the "Best Non-fiction Book of 2004" by the Book Publicists of Southern California, and has been described as the best personal experience of combat in WWII. Author is also a popular speaker around the country about these major battles to clubs and organizations and also on radio and TV.

Featured in the two best selling video games of WWII by Electronic Arts Entertainments (EA) *Medal of Honor--The Rising Sun*, and also *The Assault on Tarawa*, to describe the combat scenes that are being shown.

Also author of: *The Mysterious and Secret Order of the Knights of the Golden Circle; How To Find The Treasures of the Knights of the Golden Circle; Knights of The Golden Circle Treasure Signs; Lost Treasure Secrets;* and *Fugitives from Freedom*.

Columnist, feature story writer and staff member of following publications: *Treasure; Treasure Search; Treasure Found; Treasure Diver; Treasure Hunter; Treasure News;* and *The CB Guide magazine*.

Editor and feature writer: *Treasure Hunter Confidential* newsletter; and the *Adventures' Club News of Los Angeles* (also a member of the organization).

Contributing editor: *Biblical and American Archeologist* newsletter.

Columnist and reporter: *The Kansas City Star; Rocky Mountain Aviation magazine; Fabulous Las Vegas magazine- Stillwater News Press-* and *the O'Collegian*.

Featured in: *The Treasure of Elysian Park* on the Television Series "Unsolved Mysteries" -

-also on John Burrud's *Treasure Series*-- NBC's Special on *Diving For Spanish Treasure Galleons in Varacruz, Mexico*-- ABC's Series on *How to Find Lost Treasure* and *The Hunt for Amazing Treasures*-- The Frank Sayer Show on *The Lost Dutchman Mine*--

and *American Treasure Hunters in Search of 17 Tons of Gold*, filmed by the Tokyo Broadcasting System in 1997-- Co-Host on TV's Americas' Lost Treasures, Plus numerous other radio and television broadcasts.

Also a consultant and shown on the recent 2009, History Channel, two-hour Special: *Jesse James' Hidden Treasure*; plus consultant on the 2008 Movie; *National Treasure II, Book of Secrets* by Walt Disney/Jerry Bruckheimer Studios; and also as consultant and included on the TV documentary *The Loot of Lima*.

Ph.D in Biblical Archaeology, and BA in Journalism.

Former Professor at UCLA and Los Angeles City Colleges; also Technical Writer on Pilots Handbooks for numerous Aerospace Companies for 27 years.

Contents

Dedication
Other Credits of Dr. Roy William Roush, Ph.D. Introduction

Chapt. 1 THE MYSTERIOUS AND SECRET ORDER OF THE KNIGHTS OF THE GOLDEN CIRCLE 5
- Who They Were 5
- Their Origins 5
- The Civil War 6
- Sabotage and Spying Against The North 6
- Their Plans To Start Another War 7
- The South Shall Rise Again 7

Chapt. 2 TREASURE TO FINANCE ANOTHER CIVIL WAR 9
- Did Jesse James Hide Some Of The Treasure 9
- Did The KGC Find Old Spanish Treasures 10
- Secretly Hidden For Years 10
- Some Found By Treasure Hunters 11
- The Sentinel Who Threatened My Grandfather 12
- Some Treasures Still There 13

Chapt. 3 HOW TO FIND THEIR TREASURES 15
- Locations And Places 15
- Old Mines, Tunnels, And Cellars 15
- Secret Treasure Signs 16
- Turkey Tracks 17
- Turtle Signs 17
- Hoot Owl Trees 17
- More Than One Treasure At A Site 18
- Treasure Map Overlay 18
- Detecting Equipment Needed 18
- Beware Of Sentinels And Booby Traps 19
- Decoys 19

Chapt. 4 WAS JESSE JAMES A MEMBER OF THE KGC 23
- Attack On His Mothers Home 23
- Which Arm Was Blown Off 24
- A Southern Patriot 26
- The Man in Lawton 27

Chapt. 5 DID BOB FORD REALLY KILL JESSE JAMES 31
- Has The World Been Deceived All These Years 31
- Some Strange Things Come To Light 31

What Gun Did Bob Ford Use 32
DNA Tests Not Conclusive 32
Why Bob Ford Didn't Fear For His Life 33
Texas Attorney General Waggoner Carr, On Who Shot Charlie Bigelow............34
Claims That The Governor Was In On The Hoax 35

Chapt. 6 A JESSE JAMES TREASURE FOUND IN OKLAHOMA 41
Joe Hunter And His Mysterious Treasure Maps 41
Clues Found On Some Rocks 41
Frank James Had Searched For The Treasure 42
A Jesse James Treasure Found 42
More Clues Discovered 43
Old Brass Kettle Buried By Jesse James 43

Chapt. 7 JESSE JAMES RIDES AGAIN 49
The Meeting In Lawton 49
J Frank Dalton Claims To Be Jesse James 50
The Treasure And Their Signs Explained 50
Was He Jesse James—Or Not 51
Head Lines—Jesse James Is Alive In Lawton 53
He Said That Bob Ford Did Not Kill Him..54
Belle Starr 55
Jesse Goes On A Speaking Tour 55
He Dies In Texas In 1951 At 104 Years Of Age 56
Orvus Lee Howk Or Jesse James III 57
Some Interesting Questions 59
Frank 'Pistol Pete' Eaton 59
Did Jesse Ever Use The Name Of Dalton 60
Conclusion 61
What's In A Name 62

ADDENDUM SECTION 73
Photo Of Bob Fords Finger..76
About The Author 80

INTRODUCTION

Recently, there has been a renewed interest in two of the most interesting and intriguing subjects in America's history—that of Jesse James and also about the secretive Knights of The Golden Circle, They were a very large, rebel, Southern underground organization during the 1800's that had planned to restart the Civil War again.

But, in order to do that, they knew it would take a great amount of financing and organization; so they started to accumulate a great amount of wealth and military equipment that they secretly buried around the country for many years.

Then eventually, when they failed to start the war again, their treasures remained buried and it became America's greatest lost treasure. It has been estimated to have been worth billions of dollars, and some of it still remains there--waiting to be found.

Strangely, the story of the KGC is not mentioned in any of our modern history books. For some strange reason, it has been omitted in spite of the fact that they were well known during the late 1800's when they were the most active, and did receive a lot of nationwide publicity. But now, perhaps their story has been intentionally left out because of a lingering bias and resentment against them for their disloyalty and rebellious actions against the Union. The issue is still somewhat of a sore spot, especially among some people in the South.

Of course, most of you are already familiar with America's most famous old western outlaw, Jesse James, along with his older brother, Frank, and their notorious gang who staged some of the biggest and most violent bank and train robberies in American history.

They have also been the subject of numerous movies, television programs, books, newspaper and magazine articles for many years, and even in the old famous song "When That Dirty Little Coward Shot Mr. Howard." (That was when Jesse was living under the assumed name of Mr. Howard.)

Most historians and most Americans have believed the old conventional story that Jesse James was shot to death by Bob Ford, in April 1882 after Jesse had done a very strange thing. He 'uncustomarly' removed his two gun belts, placed them on the bed in plain sight of Bob Ford and his brother (two new members of the gang), then placed a chair against the wall and stood up on it with his back to them, presumably, to dust off a picture frame.

That doesn't sound realistic. I think Bob should have come up with a more logical and believable story if he had really killed Jesse James. I was quite young when I first heard that explanation and I thought that it sounded a little phony then--and I still do, especially after I read an article recently that told Bob Ford's personal story, word-for-word, of how he claimed it happened. Bob also mentioned in the article that even he did not notice any dust on the picture frame. The whole story is shot full of holes and just doesn't stand up.

It was well known that Jesse always wore his guns even inside his own home since he was always on the alert of being shot or ambushed, even from some of his friends or members of his own gang, especially since there was a $15,000 reward posted for him--dead or alive! So it doesn't make sense that he would unexpectedly make himself such an easy target.

However, it makes a lot more sense that the whole thing was a hoax with somebody else being killed so that Jesse could go on living under an assumed name and not being hunted by the law. It is known that Jesse was a very clever man.

An old legend claims that it was actually another person that had just joined the gang, Charlie Bigelow, who was shot and killed. Then the body was identified by the family and others who said that it was really Jesse James. That way, Bob Ford could claim the reward and Jesse could secretly live on under an assumed name. Remember, very few people really knew what Jesse looked like, so it wouldn't have been too difficult to pull it off— even to fake photographs of a supposedly dead body. I have also heard that Charlie Bigelow had a striking resemblance to Jesse James, so that would have made it even easier.

Writers of our modern history books have obviously taken the most conventional and accepted versions of whatever subject they may be writing about rather than to spend extra time doing research. Then, each time this happens, the versions get changed a bit. Consequently, a lot of actual history is really unknown to the general public.

But now, some history buffs and others are beginning to question the old traditional versions of what some of our history has led us to believe. They are digging back into some of the records and are beginning to uncover some rather interesting information as to what may have really happened—but more on that in Chapter Five.

This book also includes more information about the Knights of The Golden Circle, plus information about their hidden treasures and clues on how to look for it, plus information about Jesse James and the strong probability that he was also a member of the KGC and buried some of his stolen loot to add to their treasures.

This is my fourth book on the subject of the KGC and their treasures. The other three are: *The Mysterious And Secret Order of The Knights of The Golden Circle; How To Find The Treasures of The Knights of The Golden Circle;* and *Knights of The*

Golden Circle Treasure Signs.

Then recently, I had the honor of being a consultant and interviewed twice for the special, two-hour, History Channel Program: *"Jesse James' Hidden Treasure."*

It was first televised in November 2009. Parts of my interview were included, plus my descriptions of some scenes that were being shown. The program dealt with the history of Jesse James, The Knights of The Golden Circle Treasures, Jesses' possible association with it, and that Jesse was probably not killed by Bob Ford, but lived on under an assumed name for years.

Chapter One

THE MYSTERIOUS AND SECRET ORDER OF THE KNIGHTS OF THE GOLDEN CIRCLE

WHO THEY WERE

Not many people have ever heard of the Knights of The Golden Circle (KGC) and even fewer know why they existed because virtually nothing about them is mentioned in our modern history books today, nor was there anything mentioned about them in any of the history books when I went to school and college--and history was my favorite subject.

However, they did exist for many years, and played an important part in our politics and history, especially before and during the time of the Civil War. It's probably the greatest untold story in the history of the United States today. But during most the 1800's, this very large, powerful, and Southern rebel organization was well known and many articles about them and their bold activities were published in most of our newspapers, magazines, and periodicals; including many old reports in our National Archives.

It was never known for sure how many members they had because they eventually became a very secret and underground society, but it is estimated to have been in the hundreds of thousands.

Then after the South lost the War, they refused to accept the terms of the surrender and went underground as a very secret, even dangerous and subversive, organization with serious plans to restart the Civil War again, overthrow our Government, and divide this nation into two separate countries.

However, as time went on, the South began to economically recover and most of their devout leaders and hotheads died out and their goals became a lost cause. However, the fact remains that they did exist and were a very large and powerful organization for a long period of time.

THEIR ORIGINS

The KGC were formerly organized in 1835 (26 years before the Civil War started) as a secret organization by Senator John C. Calhoun, William Porcher and others in Lexington, Kentucky. The group was very heavy on rituals, most of which were borrowed from the Masonic Lodge, but also from the Knights of Pythias and the Rosicrucians.

Basically, they were direct descendent of older secret societies with similar ideas, including some called Sons of Liberty, Copperheads, The Lone Star, Circle of Honor, Order of American Knights and others, so their ideals had been going on for a number of years before.

One of those was a popular movement that had started long before the Civil War when our young nation was reaching out for more territory to expand our borders westward. At that time, they had bold plans of imperialism to gain more territory for our growing nation, and mostly through their efforts, Texas was brought into the Union. They even had ambitious plans to annex Cuba, and also Mexico when it was ruled by the French.

During that period of time, our entire country was pretty much united and worked together to achieve some of these goals, until the growing issue of slavery began to be a national problem and started to divide the sentiments of the North from the South. Unfortunately, a law to ban slavery could not be passed because of the opposition from the South. With the Southerners not willing to give up slavery and with the North opposing it, our nation was threatened with Civil War.

THE CIVIL WAR

Most of the KGC members were Southerners, which included many top politicians, officials and men of importance; so when the Civil War began in April 1861, they became ardent supporters of the Southern cause and against the North imposing its will against them. Open defiance of the Constitution of the United States was nothing unusual at that time in the South.

SABOTAGE AND SPYING AGAINST THE NORTH

They were very active during the Civil War and went underground with drastic and subversive measures in their efforts to aid the Confederacy. Some of the finest and craftiest brains in the South helped organize and direct the activities of the group against the North and the Union Army. This included sabotage, infiltration of the Government and spying activities. They are credited with helping some of the Confederate's military successes during the war.

They were so effective that President Lincoln once referred to them as a "Fifth Column" which might have been the original use of the term. Also, they have been strongly suspected of being involved in the plot to assassinate President Lincoln at the end of the war. We know that John Wilkes Booth, who assassinated President Lincoln, did not act alone.

They had been described as one of the deadliest, wealthiest, most secretive and efficient spy and underground organizations in the history of the world, and the original Ku Klux Klan was their military arm. Their goal was the dissolution of the Union and to establish a Southern Empire--not a Confederacy or a Republic, but an Empire.

In 1862 during the second year of the War, Charles G. Leyland wrote on page 573 in the Continental Monthly: "Nearly every man of influence in the South (and many a pretended Union Man of the North) is a member of the Knights of the Golden Circle, and sworn, under the penalty of assassination, to labor, in season and out of season, by fair means or foul, at all times, and on all occasions, for accomplishments of its objective."

THEIR PLANS TO START ANOTHER WAR

After the War was over, they were extremely bitter over the defeat of the Confederate Army and deeply resented the terms forced upon them by the unconditional surrender. They had been working diligently for many years to establish a Confederate Nation independent from the Northern States and were not about to give up yet. They wanted to regain what they had lost.

The American Civil War was noted as being especially bitter and hard fought. Feelings and resentments between the two sides were very strong and long lasting. It had literally been neighbor against neighbor, and brother against brother. Many Southerners ignored General Lee's surrender to General Sherman and didn't want the war to end. They wanted to keep fighting until they won. In fact, many of the Southern soldiers kept their arms and continued fighting for a while. Because of that, it took weeks before the fighting finally stopped. Though their army might have been beaten and gave up, the spirit of the South was still alive.

As for the KGC organization, they considered the surrender as only a temporary cease-fire, and they began very secret meetings with a strongly determined and clandestine, even bizarre, conspiracy, to eventually restart the Civil War later, at a time of their choosing.

THE SOUTH SHALL RISE AGAIN

Everyone has heard the slogan, "The South shall rise again." We smile when we hear it now, but the Southerners were really serious about it then. Following the Civil War, information about them became very scarce. However, our Government and the Secret Service knew of their activities and the dangers they posed, but evidence on them was difficult to obtain.

Then in 1874, a government secret agent by the name of James Steger, successfully infiltrated one of their cells in Kentucky and became an important member of it. He gained much information that he later turned over to the Government. That resulted in the prosecution of most of the leaders of the KGC in that state for treason, but it did little to stop or hinder the rest of the organization in other states from continuing their activities, except that they became more vigilant and secretive in their activities.

Even though their membership was in the hundreds of thousands, including many people of importance and influence, their plans eventually became a lost cause and their story got faded from our history.

That's not particularly surprising when we consider who they were and what they tried to do, which was to divide this nation into two separated countries so they could rule themselves and to continue with slavery. That was a very rebellious period in our history.

Perhaps our history should be re-written, at least to the extent that this organization did exist and the strong effect they had on our country for a long period of time.

Chapter Two

Treasure To Finance Another Civil War

It was probably during the last days of the Civil War when it appeared that the South was going to lose, that the KGC, as well as some other Southerners, decided that the surrender would only serve as a cease-fire until they could restart the war again and fight until they could win. For them, it wasn't over yet.

But they realized that in order to do that they would have to be well organized and well financed with a great amount of money and equipment to supply a new army. So they very secretly started collecting money, gold and silver bars, jewelry, arms, ammunition and other valuables in any way that they could, including stealing and robbery, then hiding it around the country.

How all of it was collected is a matter of conjecture, but probably began from their own pockets and from sympathizers, but also a lot from bank, stagecoach and train robberies, or any other means, fair or foul.

Some believe that the KGC started out with what was left of the Confederate treasury at the end of the war. Treasure hunters have been looking for years for the missing wagonloads of gold that belonged to the Confederate Treasury as it was being moved southward and was never found.

I think that the KGC used a method whereby each cell, or branch, sometimes referred to as Castles, hid treasures that they had probably collected themselves in their own territory, and then assigned armed sentinels to guard it. Also, it appears that they all, more-or-less, incorporated similar ideas and markers for burying and concealing their treasures, but no two sites were alike. Each one was an original.

I don't believe there was ever a master list of where all of these treasure sites were or any maps made of each site with instructions on how to read the signs. I think it was all committed to memory because maps and lists could be stolen or memorized, but when it came time to recover the treasures, it could be found by most any member who knew what they were looking and how to read the signs. But, if you were not a recognized KGC member, you had to be careful of the nearby sentinels. They were armed and dangerous--and some may still be out there today.

DID JESSE JAMES HIDE SOME OF THE TREASURES

There is now evidence that Jesse James and his gang, who were all devout Southerners and hated the Union with a passion, were members of the KGC and were contributing to the KGC treasures. It has been noted that the gang mostly robbed from Northern banks and interests.

When they robbed trains and stagecoaches, the money was usually in large strong boxes, making them very convenient to bury just as they were. It was a strong box that had been buried at Glorieta Pass in New Mexico (reported to have been a Union Army payroll chest full of gold coins) that I found the remains of in 1973 when I was there searching for a KGC treasure.

Also, as mentioned more in detail in Chapter Six, there is proof that one of Jesse James' treasures was found in Oklahoma, and it was claimed to have been buried as part of a KGC treasure. Other treasure hunters are still looking there for chests or boxes of treasure that Jesse and his gang buried there.

DID THE KGC FIND OLD SPANISH TREASURES

There is also reason to believe that the KGC went on some treasure hunts themselves and found some of the old Spanish gold and silver mines (including bars of gold and silver) that the Spanish had abandon and hidden around many parts of our country; and they also probably found some of the old pirate and Spanish shipwreck treasures. The amount of the Spanish treasures alone are believed to have been huge and would have greatly increased the size of the KGC treasure.

That would also explain why some modern day treasure hunters, after finding and following some of these old Spanish treasure signs, were not able to find any of the treasure itself, or would only find where it had once been, but no longer there.

SECRETLY HIDDEN FOR YEARS

Normally, you would expect their treasures to be safely stored in safes or vaults someplace and locked up, especially due to its value, but they had a much better idea than that.

Actually, it was out in the open and in plain sight all the time—at least, the many treasure signs they left around them to mark the locations were in plain sight. But the signs and markings were so clever, that unless you knew what you were looking at, you would not recognize them for what they were, and pass on by. And that is exactly what the KGC had intended. It was an ingenuous and diabolically clever method that worked for many years afterwards.

Another advantage of this system was that when the time came for their callto-arms, the funding would already be in place and available throughout the country.

The fact that they somehow managed to secretly accumulate this huge amount of treasure and supplies to finance their cause is amazing enough, but even more amazing is how they secretly hid it around the country for decades after the Civil War, right under our noses, without anyone, except them, knowing about it or what they were doing.

That was quite remarkable, especially when you consider the great amount of work and time they had to spend around these sites to not only bury the treasure, but also to place signs and markers around them. Most of these signs themselves took a lot of work and time to make.

Also, they usually had to return a few times later on to add more treasure as it became available. It was not like they secretly went out one dark night, buried their loot, quietly left and didn't come back again.

I'm sure that sometimes a few outsiders must have seen or observed some of their activities, but were not able to understand what was going on-- or if they did, they never lived to tell about it.

It was not only the nations biggest secret for many years, but also it was for the longest period of time. It was a caper much bigger than anything our CIA ever thought of.

SOME FOUND BY TREASURE HUNTERS

However, in about 1970, rumors began to spread among some of the treasure hunters about the KGC and the large amount of treasure they had been secretly buried around the country by the KGC, and also that some of it had been found.

At first, I found that rather hard to believe. In fact, I had never heard of the KGC or their treasures before. But later, I became convinced and started on my own research, as did some other treasure hunters.

It was not until the early 1970's that a few articles began to appear in "Treasure Magazine" as well as some other treasure publications about their treasures, including some reports that booby traps had killed a couple of treasure hunters that had been searching for it.

That exposed their great secret for the first time. I happened to be a writer and staff member for this magazine as well as some other treasure publications at the time. But I, as well as others, was rather skeptical of this amazing information, and if it was true, why hadn't we heard of it before.

That led to further research and a growing public interest. Now, modern researchers and historian have been uncovering much information about their activities, but most of the credit for uncovering this important part of American history belongs to the treasure hunters.

Even though the opportunity never came for them to start the war again, what they otherwise did is one of the most successful and well-planned events in our history. It was a great tribute to them--not only to acquire and hide this great amount of money and treasure, but also to keep it as a national secret for all of those years, especially considering the great number of people that were involved, which was at least several hundred thousand.

As years went by, their cause began to disintegrate and become less important. The South had pretty much recovered economically and many of the old hotheads had died off. Then we had a war with Spain in 1898 that distracted a lot of attention from their cause. But after World War One ended in 1918, our Country was pretty much united and it was obviously too late to start another Civil War. Besides, our young men who had been fighting together, had no interest in fighting each other after that.

As to how many years the KGC collected and buried their treasures is a matter of conjecture. But I would estimate that they were very active for about the first 40 years, or more, after the Civil War, and most of their treasure sites were still guarded by sentinels for many years after that. In fact, my Grandfather had been threatened by one of them in Kansas in about 1931.

THE SENTINAL WHO THREATENED MY GRANDFATHER

That happened when my Grandfather had discovered that the fence line on his farm that he had purchased in about 1928 in eastern Kansas, did not enclose a small corner of the property line. So, when he went out to change the fence to include it, a man who lived nearby that we did not know, came over and told him that if he changed the fence line, he would shoot him.

But a few months later, my Grandfather returned with my Dad (both well armed), plus myself as a youngster, and we changed the fence line without any more threats. We didn't know anything about the man except that he kept to himself, also that he did not own the adjoining property. It was also strange that he didn't farm or raise any cattle. So, we could never figure out why he would be so threatening—that was, not until a few years ago when I happened to visit the property and discovered a lot of KGC treasure signs that were still there, plus a big hole where the treasure had been dug up with a backhoe.

Unfortunately, we had sold the property in about 1944 and the treasure along with it. Obviously, the threatening man was the sentinel and probably had secretly dug up the treasure sometime later. The house where the man had lived also was no longer there.

This site on my Grandparents farm is where I spent all my summer vacations during grade school. For many years, I hunted, fished and played many times over the entire area where all the numerous treasure signs were--even over the treasure itself, but none of us saw anything out of the ordinary. Actually, the area was a favorite spot for us to spend some extra time around since it was rather scenic, with a small waterfall, lots of timber, big rocky bluffs, and good fishing.

How ironic it seems now! If only I had known then what I know now! And it just goes to prove that here was one example where their treasure sites and signs were out in the open for everyone to see for years without it being recognized or discovered.

SOME TREASURES STILL THERE

The big question though, is what eventually happened to all of the KGC treasures after the turn of the century? No one really knows, but I think it was pretty much up to the sentinels to decide because by then very few of the other members knew where the sites were, nor how to understand the signs.

But the sentinels also had a problem. They were under threat of death if they took the treasure themselves, or failed to guard it properly, and wondered if there were still secret members around who were watching them? They didn't know for sure.

However, I'm sure that many of the sentinels died and took their secrets with them to the grave. In other cases, their sons or other relatives took over the job, and years later, some of them eventually helped themselves to the treasures. But there was still enough left to be found by some modern-day treasure hunters.

What they did, how they did it and how they had kept it a secret for such a long period of time is amazing. It was a real credit to them because the idea of accumulating a great treasure for their purpose, then successfully hiding it all around the country, in plain sight, and undiscovered for all those years, was one of the most well-planned and executed events in our history.

Amazing…unbelievable…Of course, it may sound that way, but who they were and what they did is a matter of record that is substantiated in many old newspaper articles and other publications during the 1800's and later.

Chapter Three

HOW TO FIND THEIR TREASURES

LOCATIONS AND PLACES

Most of their treasures were hidden in the Southern part of the United States, especially in the Southeast, but also virtually in every state from coast to coast, and especially in our gold and silver mining areas.

In other places, holes were dug for smaller cashes and cleverly concealed, then armed sentinels were assigned, under threat of death if they failed, to protect them from being found.

They seemed to prefer certain locations, like ones that were close to prominent places or landmarks that were likely to remain and could be found and identified years later, such as unusual geological formations, old mines, old forts, old trails and roads, battlefields, cemeteries, even false graves, but they could be located most anyplace.

OLD MINES, TUNNELS, AND CELLARS

As their valuables were collected, some were secretly buried in old mines and tunnels, or maybe in a natural cave or pit, with the entrance carefully hidden. Another favorite hiding place was in wells and old food cellars, then covered over and hidden.

Also, I have heard that sometimes KGC treasures were hidden in attics and basements, which would have been a quick and easy place to store items and also to watch over them at the same time. When searching in rooms or other dwellings, always check for false walls or flooring.

Another possibility would have been in the walls or floors of old dugout dwellings. These would have been a natural place to hide treasure in, especially after they were abandoned because of the large vacant hole that was left.

These dugouts were rather common in the early days of settling the West, especially out in the prairie regions where wood and other building materials were scarce. Here, Pioneers would dig a rectangular room about seven or eight feet deep, then add on about three feet of wood above to make windows, then add a roof and put about eight or 10-inches of soil over that.

They were quick, cheap and relatively easy to make. Also they were well insulated, being cool in the summer and warm in the winter. They had steps leading down to them just like the old fruit cellars had. But the roof was an attraction for the cattle so they had to put a fence around the top to keep them off.

I remember seeing some of these dugouts with people still living in them in the Panhandle area of Oklahoma in the early part of the 1930's during the drought and depression years. Later, one of them was preserved as a historic attraction for a while.

SECRET TREASURE SIGNS

It was very important to put signs around to mark each of their treasure sites. But it was of critical importance to do that in such a way that they would usually not stand out from their surroundings, and would instead, blend into it so they could not be recognized for what they really were, or why they were placed there. They were meant to not attract attention, but to be thought of as just another rock, another tree, or some markings of no importance.

Probably their most common signs were hand-carved stones that were in a variety of sizes and shapes that were scattered around their sites. They could be anywhere from about six-inches to several feet in size. Some were shaped like a diamond, others like a square, a rectangle, a boot, an arrowhead, etc., but don't be fooled by arrowheads or other pointers. Some were meant to purposely lead you in the opposite direction.

Beyond that, there might be holes drilled into rocks, trees, cliffs, etc. as pointers that you would have to figure out what they mean. Normally, there was never an "X" directly over the treasure itself, but it would usually be where two or more lines-of-sight would cross, or where something was missing in a pattern that should be there.

No two sites were the same. That was protection in case some outsider happened to find one of their treasures, then he could not use the identical way to find another. Each site was unique and blended into the terrain.

Some of their signs had a special meaning, while others did not. That was part of their clever plan. It was up to whoever was supposed to come back later for the treasure to figure out which signs were useful and what they meant.

For example, at the site I discovered a few years ago on the old farm in Kansas, there were a few rocks that resembled a fish--and they were smiling. Later, I realized that the fish rocks had meant to look for the treasure near the water, because that is where I discovered where the treasure had been-- next to a running stream.

A point of interest is that with all of their signs, markings and shaped rocks around their treasure sites, nowhere did they ever write or use the words "KGC" or "Knights of The Golden Circle" anywhere that I know of. Nor did they leave any notes or claims of ownership to the site. Protection of the site was left personally to the sentinels.

Other signs I have seen were faces that were carved or scratched on rocks or on the side of a cliff, Most of the faces that I have seen were smiling and also were looking towards where the treasure was.

TURKEY TRACKS

Sometimes, you might see what are called "Turkey Tracks." These are marks that resembled bird tracks, and sometimes are shown walking towards the treasure site, or sometimes away from it, or maybe towards the next sign that you need to see and follow.

TURTLE SIGNS

Some signs may be in the shape of a turtle or a turtles' head. Turtle signs were also often used by the Spanish as markers for their old mines and buried treasures, so it's possible that these locations may be where the KGC discovered something the Spanish had buried, then converted it to one of their own treasure locations and left the turtle signs there.

HOOT OWL TREES

Since most of their signs and markers were relatively small and not noticeable unless someone was within a few feet of them, the KGC usually put up what have are termed "Hoot Owl Trees" that were visible from further away. They would be the first indication that you were approaching one of their sites, provided you could recognize them for what they were.

These trees were bent, grafted, or deformed into strange and bazaar shapes when they were small and flexible. Some were bent or bowed into 90-degree angles, or into other strange shapes. Sometimes, two trees were grafted together as the base to form a "V" shape. These were usually meant to sight through, like a gun sight, towards another sign that you need to see and follow next.

Hoot Owl trees would also make the location a little casier to find years later in case the terrain changed or their other signs got covered up with overgrowth. So usually, they chose placers where there were trees and rocks to bury most of their treasures.

I have noticed at several locations that some of their Hoot Owl Trees were a bit smaller and younger than some of the others around them. I believe that is because the sentinels not only had the duty of guarding the treasure, but also to maintain their treasure signs so that if some of the trees died or got destroyed, he would replace them.

MORE THAN ONE TREASURE AT A SITE

It is believed that usually there were more than just one treasure buried at most sites. Obviously, not all of their treasure and equipment was available when they started, so they kept adding to their sites as more was acquired. That makes a lot of sense, especially considering the great amount of labor and man-hours it took to prepare each site. Also, fewer sentinels would be needed.

TREASURE MAP OVERLAY

As an aid to look for these additional treasures, some treasure hunters are using the overlay map that is printed on the front cover of my second book, *"HOW TO FIND THE TREASURES OF THE KNIGHTS OF THE GOLDEN CIRCLE."*

It was submitted by a treasure hunter to *"THE TREASURE HUNTER CONFIDENTIAL NEWSLETTER"* a few years ago while I was co-editor of the publication. Though I never had the opportunity to try it out, I've heard that at some locations, it can be helpful.

If you are looking for their treasure and you happen to recognize one of their sites, I think the best advice would be to first, find the perimeters of it. This could be done by walking around it in all four directions until you find no more shaped rocks or other signs, then the treasure should be located somewhere near the center of the area.

DETECTING EQUIPMENT NEEDED

It is essential to have a good metal detector and the knowledge on how to use it properly, otherwise, you are wasting a lot of time and effort. Most detectors with standard-sized, 10-inch-loops should be adequate, however, other detecting devices can be useful, such as ground penetration radar and other specially designed equipment.

The KGC used a variety of items to put their valuables in, such as glass jars, cooking pots, iron kettles, old plunger-type butter churns, barrels, boxes, chests and trunks. It was the remains a military type pay chest that I had found at Glorieta Pass, New Mexico in 1973, and also the remains of a small empty trunk that I found on the old Dalton property near Tulsa, Oklahoma in about 1979. Normally they preferred items that would not rust away. Also, rust might stain what was inside. But they often did bury miscellaneous pieces of iron as hidden markers, such as pick heads.

BEWARE OF SENTINELS AND BOOBY TRAPS

However, a word of caution! After all of these years, do not assume that the treasure is unguarded, or is not booby-trapped. Just recently, I heard of one location back East that is still being guarded by an elderly and unfriendly old man who totes a big rifle and warns people to stay away from his land. It's also reported that the man seems to always have a lot of money to spend.

Whether he may be one of the last assigned sentinels, or maybe someone who just happened to have discovered treasure on his land, or just an old grouch, it adds up to the same thing--Beware! Even other treasure hunters can sometimes be dangerous, and I have seen a few of them out there.

DECOYS

Another clever thing they did to protect their treasures was to use decoys so that if found, they would mislead someone into thinking the treasure was already gone, or had not been buried yet.

A perfect example was one that I found with my metal detector at Glorieta Pass in New Mexico. After I had figured out exactly where to dig, I got an excellent signal from my metal detector right on the spot. Excitedly, I dug down about two feet and discovered an old black powder can made of tin. But, to my disappointment, it was empty. At first, I thought what I was supposed to think... that the treasure was gone, and give up.

Then I realized the situation, removed the can and started to dig down further. I could also see that the ground below it had once been disturbed and filled back in. So, I stared digging again.

But since the site was just a couple of feet from the edge of a large dry wash, I discovered that a recent big flood had undercut the embankment and washed out the treasure. Later, we heard that it had been accidentally found a few months before, and the guy had become wealthy. If only I had been there sooner!

At one time, the treasures of the KGC had to be Americas' greatest lost treasure—and maybe still is. Some have estimated its value to have been in the billions of dollars.

As to how much of the treasure is still out there is only a matter of a guess, but I would estimate somewhere between one-fourth to a third of it-- and is the stuff that dreams are made of to treasure hunters.

This is a typical looking "Hoot Owl" that the author (left) found at a KGC treasure site in New Mexico. The tree was bent into this position when it was very small and flexible to serve as a marker that a treasure was buried nearby. The direction of the bend would usually be in a line-of-sight either towards the treasure, or in the opposite direction. In this case, it pointed away from the treasure; however the treasure was no longer there, but the outline of an army pay chest was still clearly visible.

Chapter Four

WAS JESSE JAMES A MEMBER OF THE KNIGHTS OF THE GOLDEN CIRCLE

In addition to numerous claims that Jesse and others in the gang were members of the KGC, there are also logical reasons to believe that they were, including reports that Jesse had associations with known members of the KGC. There is no doubt that the gang were all loyal Southerners and to the cause of the Confederates, and one of the best ways to do that was to join and help the KGC.

However, I doubt if he or any other members of the gang attended many lodge meetings due to their circumstances of hiding out or being on the run most of the time to different places, but if Jesse or some of the others were members, then they were more like free-lance members.

Jesse and his brother, Frank, had fought with Quantrill's Raiders against the North during the War. Quantrill was known as a guerrilla leader who was particularly brutal. They were more like an armed bunch of vigilantes that carried out attacks in Missouri and Eastern Kansas. They ransacked and plundered the areas they invaded. Could some of their booty have been added to the KGC treasures later? It's very likely.

It is known that Jesse and his brother hated the Union and were very loyal to the South. One reason is because the law and the Pinkertons had pursued both of them relentlessly after the War, and had put a big reward out for Jesse's capture-- dead or alive, making his life very difficult and precarious.

ATTACK ON HIS MOTHER'S HOME

Also, his mother's home had been attacked by Pinkerton Agents one night. They were looking for Jesse and Frank who supposedly were not there at the time. At least, that is according to one version of the incident, but if they were, then they escaped during the confusion.

The agents tossed a lighted flare through a window, but it soon exploded, killing his seven-year-old half-brother, blowing off the lower part of one of his mother's arms, knocking his step-father unconscious, plus doing extensive damage to the house.

WHICH ARM WAS BLOWN OFF

Incidentally, that brings up a very interesting question. Which arm of his mother was partially blown off--her right, or her left? There is a disagreement and controversy still going on over that issue today—but there is a way of telling which arm it really was!

It has been stated in some books and articles that it was definitely her right arm because in at least two different photos of her (such as the one photo of her in this book) it clearly shows part of her right arm missing. However, in some of the other photos of her, it appears that it is her left arm. Why the strange difference?

An explanation to the apparent inconsistency is that there were numerous photos of her that were taken over the years. The earlier ones were "Tintypes" which show things in reverse, while later photos of her were taken with film cameras that show images correctly.

Tintypes show things in reverse, like looking into a mirror, because each one is an original and was the actual light-sensitive plate used in the rear of the old-fashion cameras to capture the image. All photos up until the use of film, and even later, were Tintypes. I have a few old family Tintypes that were taken back during that period of time and they are actually made of tin and are sepia tone in color.

It was not until 1885 that George Eastman discovered how to use film for taking pictures so images could be seen correctly—not opposite of what they really were.

So, if the old photos of Jesse's mother were from original Tintypes, that show it was her right arm missing, then actually, it was her left arm that was blown off.

But sometimes there were exceptions to that situation, and that was when printers happened to realize this oddity of Tintypes, and printed them in reverse in order to show them correctly. Otherwise, Tintypes were misleading.

That situation with Tintypes has created a lot of errors among historians and the public for years.

One example of this is with some of the portraits of a young Jesse James (like the one on the front of this book) that shows him looking to his right, while others you may see of this same photo, show him looking to his left.

Which way he is really looking we may never know for sure, unless someone has the original Tintype of that pose.

Another example is of Billy The Kid. He was traditionally thought of as a "Left-Handed-Gun" because of the famous tintype picture of him with a revolver on his left hip and holding a rifle in his right hand.

But if you look closely, you can see that the breach of the rifle is on the wrong side, proving that it's a Tintype, and is shown in reverse. Rifles never had the breach on the left side.

Also, in 1958 a feature movie was made about Billy The Kid, called "The Left Handed Gun" staring Paul Newman, but the movie makers made a big error —Billy was really right-handed. The movie was made before it became common knowledge about Tintypes that when printed, needed to be shown in reverse, and now, most printers are doing that.

But, getting back to Jesse's Mother, Mrs. Samuels. Some of the books that I have on Western Outlaws and History show a number of different pictures of her taken over the years after one of her arms was missing. Some were Tintypes and were taken around 1875. Some are shown in reverse, as taken, while others were reversed when printed.

However, there are sometimes a sure way to tell if a Tintype picture has been reversed, or shown as they originally were--and that is if you can see buttons on a coat, jacket or a blouse.

Men's apparel always have buttons on the right side, while women's are always on the left side. If they are not shown that way, like in a few examples of the pictures of Jesse's mother, then it's an old Tintype and you are seeing things in reverse.

So, there are at least two photos of her that settles the question, once and for all! These two clearly show the buttons being on the right side of her jacket, like a man's jacket. But since she is not really wearing a man's jacket, then the photo is a Tintype and is shown in reverse, showing her right arm damaged—therefore, it was part of her 'left arm' that was missing.

A SOUTHERN PATRIOT

Though Jesse was mostly considered an outlaw, there were many people in the South who liked him and considered him a hero and a Southern political figure, so he had a lot of public support in certain places

It was publicly known that he often gave money to people who needed it, or who had befriended him. He seemed to have a soft spot for the underdog, or people in trouble. He was often referred to as "The American Robin Hood." He blamed the North for the problems of the South and felt justified in trying to do something about it. Even President Truman, another Missourian, is once to have said that: "He stole from the rich and gave to the poor."

Jesse had not planned on being an outlaw after the war. But there were strong resentments on both sides for a few years afterwards. There were still old scores to settle, mainly against the Confederates and especially those who had been part of Quantrill's Raiders. So, Jesse was on the receiving end of some of them. Though he tried to live peaceable afterwards, he found that he had to defend himself—and finally turned to violence.

Since Jesse had such a high profile as an outlaw and obviously very prejudice against the North, he undoubtedly would have been sought out to join and help the KGC.

Another reason to believe that Jesse and some of his gang were members of the KGC is because, according to some reports, they stole a lot more money than they ever spent or accounted for. Jesse and the others were never known as big spenders, and there are many stories in places around the country where they had buried their ill-gotten loot, but no stories of them ever coming back to retrieve it. The most logical explanation is that they had buried it as part of the KGC treasure to be used later.

There is also information in the following chapter from an article written by the former Texas Attorney General, Waggoner Carr, who was hired to represent some people who claimed to be descendents of Jesse James. Mr. Carr states that Jesse and Frank and other members of the gang were definitely members of the KGC, and that they buried a lot of their stolen loot for the KGC.

THE MAN IN LAWTON

Then there is information in Chapter Seven about the 100-year-old man who came to Lawton, Oklahoma in June of 1948. He claimed that he was the real Jesse James, and that he had not been killed by Bob Ford, but was still alive! He said that he had been living peaceable in Texas for years under the assumed name of J. Frank Dalton.

He claimed that he had indeed been a member of the KGC and had buried a lot of stolen money for them. Some did not believe that he was really Jesse James, but there are some reasons to believe that maybe he was, and if so, that is further evidence that Jesse and some of his gang were members of the KGC.

That surprising event in Lawton had happened because of a feature story in the Lawton Newspaper about a Jesse James treasure that had been found in Oklahoma a few years before by a treasure seeker by the name of Joe Hunter. Joe was sure there was still more of it to be found, so he went to the newspaper and told his story in hopes of gaining more information from someone.

It was in response to his newspaper story that the old man came to Lawton to meet Joe Hunter and tell him more about the treasure, plus other treasures that he said he knew about--and the rest is history.

Again, credit should be given to the inquisitive nature and activities of treasure hunters for bringing to light this surprising event that astonished the world, and may rewrite part of American History.

This is Jesses' mother, Zerelda Samuels, showing that part of her <u>left arm</u> was blown off (not her right arm as erroneously stated before.) It appears here that her right arm was damaged, but since this is a tintype photo, it shows things in reverse, including the buttons on her dress. Buttons on a woman's' dress are always on the left side, while men's are always on the right side. The incident happened during a Pinkerton raid one night when a flare was tossed through her window--but it exploded. They were looking for Jesse and Frank, but they were not there at the time.

Jesse James was the most wanted man in America for a number of years and there were remarkably huge rewards out for him-- dead or alive. Also, there were rewards out for his brother or any other known member of his gang.

Chapter Five

Did Bob Ford Really Kill Jesse James

Perhaps one of the biggest hoaxes in our history that has been going on for well over a century is the story that Jesse James was shot and killed by Bob Ford in April 1882. As I said in the first part of this book, I have always thought that the story sounded unlikely, a bit phony, and made up. Now, I believe it even less, especially if we look again at the story a little closer with some logic and also at some of the new information that has come to light in the last few years. Then you can decide for yourself.

HAS THE WORLD BEEN DECEIVED ALL THESE YEARS

Obviously, some one was shot, killed, and buried. The traditional story says that it was Jesse James who was killed by Bob Ford for the reward money--but was it really Jesse James that was killed? I think not! In fact, maybe Bob Ford didn't shoot anybody.

I tend to more agree with the information that has appeared in numerous articles and books over the past few years that it was more likely, Charlie Bigelow, a new member of the gang that Jesse didn't trust and was about ready to get rid of anyway. But there are a number of additional reasons why it appears that Jesse James was not killed by Bob Ford.

SOME STRANGE THINGS HAVE COME TO LIGHT

For one thing, when the body that was exhumed in 1995 for the purpose of DNA testing from the grave in Kearney, Missouri where the body of Jesse was supposed to have been buried, some strange and unexpected things were discovered that can not be explained.

To begin with, they found that the skull was badly shattered, yet the photo that was taken, supposedly of Jesse after he was supposedly killed, does not show any evidence of a shattered skull—only a small black spot on his forehead where the bullet supposedly came out.

The photo could have been of Jesse, but if so, I doubt if he was really dead. It would not have been too difficult to arrange with a photographer to take photos of Jesse playing dead. Or it might possibly be that of Charlie Bigelow, or some one else who had a resemblance to Jesse.

WHAT GUN DID BOB FORD USE

There is something more to consider. Bob Ford claimed that he had used a .44 caliber revolver, then later, he said it was a .45 caliber revolver—but when the body that was buried in Jesse James' grave in Missouri that was exhumed in 1995, a .38 caliber bullet was found in the skull. So what is the real story? Something doesn't add up!

Also, according to a photograph in one book that I have on Western History, it shows a hole in the wall were souvenir hunters had dug out the bullet that supposedly had killed Jesse. So, did Bob Ford use a .38 or a .44 or a .45; or was the skull badly shattered, or not, and did the bullet remain in the skull, or did it end up in the wall? Why so many inconstancies? Maybe it's because Bob Ford couldn't get his made-up story straight.

Another suspicious part of the story is why did Jesse stand up on a chair to reach the picture frame? It was a small room with a very low ceiling. He could have reached it without using a chair. It also seems strange and unlikely that Jesse would choose a time like that to dust off a picture frame since it was supposed to have been a short meeting with Bob Ford and his brother regarding some business—not a social meeting.

Oddly enough, the body in the casket in Missouri was found upside down. Could that have been so that no one could see the face and recognize it as not belonging to Jesse James?

DNA TEST NOT CONCLUSIVE

According to reports, the DNA taken from the body did not conclusively match with the people who said they were living relatives of Jesse James-- the ones who had asked for the DNA to be taken.

It would not have been difficult for another person to have been killed, such as Charlie Bigelow, and claim that the body was that of Jesse James. For one thing, very few people in the area knew what Jesse really looked like, except his immediate family and some of his gang. And don't forget— who ever it was that was killed had a beard; and so did Jesse, so that would have made it easier to claim that the dead person was really Jesse.

According to one report, the corner was having difficulty trying to positively identify the body, so he sent for Jesses' mother to come, and when she first arrived, she looked at the body and said that it was not her son. But other members of the family quickly took her aside and explained the situation. Then she asked for another look, and then she said: "Yes, that is my son."

WHY BOB FORD DIDN'T FEAR FOR HIS LIFE

If Bob Ford had really killed Jesse, why didn't Jesses' brother Frank, or some other loyal members of the gang go after Bob to kill him; especially Cole Younger or one of Cole's two bothers. They were first cousins of Jesse and Frank since their mother's had been sisters. Cole was especially known as impetuous, hot-tempered, and a cold-blooded killer; and also as one of Jesses' best friends and a long-time companion. Can you imagine that would be acceptable to any of them and they wouldn't even try to get revenge? I think not!

They all had plenty of opportunities to do that since Bob had gone on a speaking tour afterwards and apparently never feared for his life, nor are there any reports that he was threatened or went into hiding. Revenge killings were quite common then, especially among the James gang and others. Bob would have been easy to find and kill, if Jesse's brother Frank or the other loyal members of the gang had wanted to. I think that alone should be convincing enough that Bob did not shoot Jesse James; and that issue seems to have never been addressed by any historians or writers yet.

The simple explanation as to why they didn't do that is because they all knew that it had been a hoax and to Jesse's advantage. There were also many people over the years who said that they knew that Jesse wasn't dead, but was still alive. It was almost an open secret. In fact, there were many newspaper stories at the time saying that Jesse was still alive and that the whole thing had been a "Put up."

Another thing to consider…If Bob Ford had really assassinated Jesse as he said he did, then he must have been a very brave and courageous man--or else very stupid. Think for a minute and put yourself in his place.

Would you have the nerve to really pull a gun on Jesse James—the notorious, cold-blooded killer, and one of the greatest gunmen in our history? Even if you did succeed in killing him, or even took a shot at him and missed, what do you think your chances would be of getting away with it? That really would be asking for trouble and be very risky business. Very few men would have taken a chance like that, and I don't think that Bob Ford was one of them.

Jesse was feared by everyone. It was said that no man could get the drop on him, and many people had died trying to do that. Jesse was always very watchful and suspicious of about everybody. He was quick on the draw and said that he would never be taken alive.

Jesse once told a friend: "If three men move in front of me, I will take all three before I fall."

Jesse owned and carried numerous guns from time-to-time. Normally, he carried two revolvers in holsters when he traveled or left the house—and even inside his house. At one time he owned a .45 caliber Colt, a .45 caliber Smith & Wesson, a beach-loading, bouble-barreled, shotgun, and a Winchester Rifle. It was also very common to carry a small concealed Derringer.

I would think that at the sound of a hammer being pulled back, Jesse would have reacted very quickly and ducked down out of the way. But according to the story he apparently just stood there. That, and other parts of the story, don't seem logical.

If I had been in Bob's place and decided to shoot Jesse under those circumstances, I would have shot him in the back once or twice to disable him, then maybe aim for his head. The logic is that the body is a much bigger target and much easier to hit than the head. So why would anyone take a chance like that with a good possibility of missing, especially with a handgun? To have shot Jesse right through the center of the head with a quick, first shot would have been a very lucky shot!

TEXAS ATTORNEY GENERAL WAGGONER CARR ON WHO REALLY SHOT CHARLIE BIGELOW

Then there is a very interesting article published in 1999 in the Texas Co-op Power Publication, which has a much more believable version of Bob Ford and Jesse James. It claims that Jesse himself had killed Charlie Bigelow who had once been his friend, but had been robbing banks and killing people, then blaming it on Jesse. So, Jesse made up his mind to get rid of Charlie, which he did—then lived on peaceable after that, using many aliases and avoiding the law. The information that Jesse himself shot Charlie Bigelow was also mentioned in one of the noted biographies about Jesse James.

If that is true, then it could explain the curious story and the inconsistencies that Bob Ford told of how he had shot Jesse--because he really hadn't!

The article was written by Waggoner Carr, a former Texas Attorney General, who had represented some people in court who said that they were descendants of Jesse James.

The story goes on to say that in 1882, the new Governor of Missouri, Tom Crittendon, had offered a $10,000 reward for Jesse because when Crittendon was campaigning for governor, he vowed that if elected, he would rid the State of bandits. That meant that Jesse was in trouble.

However, it just so happened that Jesse had been a friend and campaign contributor to Crittendon. It must be remembered that to many people in the South, Jesse wasn't an ordinary criminal. Many considered him more like a hero due to his support of the South and his fight against the North. He was often well respected, even supported, and had a lot of friends--ones who often gave him and Frank food and shelter when they were on the run.

Then, according to the article, Jesse came up with an idea. Since he was tired of being chased by the law and since he also wanted to get rid of Charlie Bigelow, he arranged for a secret meeting with the new Governor one night in the woods near his house. Jesse then had three of his friends hiding nearby so that they also could see and hear what was being said.

CLAIMS THAT THE GOVENOR WAS IN ON THE HOAX

They claimed the Governor agreed that if Jesse killed Bigelow and had him buried as Jesse James, then Jesse could leave the State, take on an assumed name and become law-abiding. That way, the Governor could keep his vow, Jesse could get rid of Bigelow and also escape from the law. It was a win-win situation.

After that, it said that Jesse went on to live around the country, mostly in Texas and free from the law by using many aliases, including J. Frank Dalton.

Also strangely enough, after only two years in jail, Frank James received a pardon from the Governor for all of the shootings, robberies, and violence that he had been involved in.

I have always thought that this pardon was unusually generous, but maybe, the Governor knew something that the public didn't know.

Following that, Frank moved to Oklahoma where he spent years trying to locate a treasure of gold bars that the gang had once buried there in the Ozark Mountains in the Southwestern part of the State. But unfortunately, most of the area had been settled and it had erased some of the old landmarks that Frank was looking for. However, that treasure was found later during the 1940's by a treasure hunter named Joe Hunter. But more about that is told in the last chapter of this book.

Also, it has been said that Bob Ford never received the reward money that had been posted for anyone who killed Jesse James. Was that because the Governor knew that he really had not killed Jesse?

So, if this information is correct, and Jesse himself shot Charlie Bigelow (or maybe it was someone else who was using the alias of Bigelow) then that could explain the rather strange story that Bob Ford told about how he had shot Jesse, since he had really had not done the shooting.

Incidentally, if some one had been killed with a direct shot to the middle of the head with a handgun, that sounds more like a shot that Jesse himself would have made.

Another possibility is that perhaps if Jesse had really killed Charlie Bigelow for some reason, it might have been then that he got the idea of saying the body was really himself.

Wagner Carr also stated that he had heard an audiotape of an early CBS radio program where the three friends who had heard the conversation that night between Jesse and the Governor were being interviewed about the incident, and each one confirmed the story.

Carr also said that he had seen and carefully researched thousands of documents, photos, newspaper articles, and family letters, plus sworn affidavits from people that said J. Frank Dalton and Jesse James were the same person, and that he was convinced of that.

When you consider the status and experience of a person like Wagner Carr, his information has to be taken seriously.

The article also said that Jesse was a member of the KGC, and that he and his gang had buried a lot of money for the organization. They considered the money was not theirs to spend, but belonged to the KGC and their effort to restart the War.

The money was buried deep and each person involved took an oath that if anyone told where the money was buried, the others had the right to kill him. Carr also said he believes that most of the treasure is still buried.

Another reason to think that Jesse was not killed by Bob Ford is told in the next chapter about J. Frank Dalton who appeared in Lawton, Oklahoma in 1948, as a very old man, claiming that he was really Jesse James, the old outlaw. And there are many reasons to maybe think that he really was— including some events that I was personally involved in much later.

Incidentally, after Bob Ford had toured the country for a while, making public appearances and bragging about how he had shot Jesse James, he moved to Creed, Colorado where he owned a saloon. One night, on 8 June 1892, he was shot to death by Ed O'Kelly over a dispute regarding the operation of his saloon. Ed used both barrels of a shotgun at close range. Then he bragged how he had killed the man who had shot Jesse James.

A few years later, on 13 January 1904 in Oklahoma City, Ed got into a scuffle with a police officer, named Joe Barnett, and when Ed pulled a gun, the officer shot him to death. He was soon forgotten and lies buried in a potter's field in Oklahoma City.

So, the officer is the man who shot the man who shot the man who said he had shot Jesse James. It was similar to Jack McCall who had shot Wild Bill Hickok in Deadwood City, South Dakota in 1885, who was later killed by someone who could brag that he had shot the man who had shot Wild Bill.

As is so often the case—violence breeds violence, and it is still going on today. Some things never seem to change.

This is the house in St. Joseph, Missouri where Jesse and his family were living when he was supposedly shot in the back of his head by Bob Ford on April 3, 1882. It supposedly happened in the room on the left. The house was very small.

This is the last photo of Cole Younger shortly before his death in 1916 at age 72. It shows what appears to be a very friendly and peaceful man. But looks are deceiving in this case because he had led a very violent life. (He had 17 bullets still in his body when he died.) He was known for his quick temper and for killing many innocent people during bank robberies. He was a main member of the James/Younger gang, along with his two brothers. He would have surely killed Bob Ford in revenge for assassinating Jesse James unless he knew the whole thing was a hoax to help Jesse escape from the law.

Chapter Six

A Jesse James Treasure Found In Oklahoma

JOE HUNTER AND HIS MYSTERIOUS TREASURE MAPS

A man by the name of Joe Hunter in Lawton, Oklahoma was unexpectedly given two treasure maps in 1933 by an old man who was a friend of his father. The man, who said that his name was Cook, told Joe that they were maps to a treasure that Jesse James and his gang had once buried in Oklahoma, but that he (himself) was no longer able to search for it, but hoped that Joe could find it.

He added: "We buried that gold there in the Wichita Mountains about 62 years ago."

Apparently, he had been a member of the James gang, but was going under an assumed name.

That turned Joe into a treasure hunter on a long search for treasure.

A few years later, Joe was given two more treasure maps that had been discovered in the false bottom of a trunk. The two maps were reportable made by Jesse James. The maps had strange markings on them, and Joe soon realized that these two maps coincided with the other two maps that he already had since they all four seemed to describe the same treasure trail.

Through further research, Joe discovered that the James gang had used a system of marks and codes, and that some of them were the same as the Old Spanish treasure signs and symbols. (That is important and it supports my belief that members of the KGC had searched for and found some of the Old Spanish treasures to add to their own treasure hoard.)

As Joe found out later, the last two maps had indeed been made by Jesse James and his gang.

So, with the help of the treasure maps, Joe went on a 15-year-long treasure hunt in the Wichita's. But the maps were not easy to understand. They were full of marks and codes that were hard to figure out.

CLUES FOUND ON SOME ROCKS

After a long search, Joe found his first clue in the Wichita Mountains—a rock on which another map had been carved.

Soon after that, Joe happened to read in the newspaper that a rock had been found on a woman's ranch north-east of Lawton, near Cement, Oklahoma with strange markings on it, He thought it must have something to do with the Jesse James treasure that he was looking for--so he went to the ranch and met the woman.

The woman then told him that years before, an old man had come to her ranch and asked her if she would show him the old spring. When they got there, the stranger said that if that was the right place, then that was Jesses' kitchen. Then he reached underneath a rock and pulled out an old spoon.

FRANK JAMES HAD SEARCHED FOR THE TREASURE

Then he asked her if she knew of a certain rock that had strange markings on it. She said that she did not. With that, the man left, but before he did, he told her that he was Frank James, Jesses' brother. That surprised the woman very much.

It is known that Frank bought a home nearby at Fletcher and lived there for many years—presumably to still hunt for the treasure. He finally died in 1915 in Oklahoma.

Later, when the woman happened to discover the rock that Frank James had been looking for 28 years before, she figured that it must be connected to treasure, and that maybe she needed some help to figure out the markings on it. That is when she told the story to the local newspaper about the rock that Joe had read.

Joe was sure that it had to do with treasure and immediately set to work to figure out the code.

A JESSE JAMES TREASURE FOUND

The information eventually led Joe to dig up a cache of Jesse James treasure worth a small fortune. It consisted of gold bullion, a quantity of jewels, and some old coins that he gave to the woman, but there was an old large, key-winder, gold watch, that he kept for his troubles.

The watch was valued at $5,000 because of its historical significance. This type of watch was the first of the pocket watches. It was the same kind of watch that I happened to find with a metal detector on Mona Island in 1986 while I was there a couple of times searching for pirate treasure. Only the case was left, but it was still a valuable and historic find.

Mona Island was considered a Pirate Capital for about 200 years. All of the

Caribbean Pirates had hung out there. It is located in the Mona Passage about 26 miles west of Puerto Rico. It is still a remote, desolate, virtually uninhabited, and dangerous place to go. It is full of large caves and other dangers, including large and hungry iguanas up to six-feet long, or longer, and about the size of small alligators. They are the largest iguanas in the Western Hemisphere and are attracted to visitors. One must be careful trying to feed them because they don't know the difference between a hand, and a hand-out. They will sometimes leap towards your hand and take the whole thing!

MORE CLUES DISCOVERED

Joe then decided that according to the maps, there was more treasure to be found. As he was digging around about two years later, he uncovered an old pick head. The handle had rotted away, but he thought the direction it pointed to was significant. Then he dug up another old pick head nearby with the handle also rotted off. Again, Joe thought the directions that the handles pointed to were significant—and they were. Buried picks or pick heads were very typical of signs that were left by the KGC.

I think it's remarkable that Joe was able to find all of those items back then without a metal detector because that was long before metal detectors were available. They didn't come on the market until about 1957, so he must have done a lot of exploratory digging. But imagine what he might have missed, and what else he might have found if he had used one.

However, Joe might have used a probe rod. Before metal detectors came into use, probe rods could be used rather effectively. In the mid 1930's, I watched 'Revenuers' looking for bottles of booze buried in a neighbor's back yard in Oklahoma City. We could smell the stuff for several days afterwards.

OLD BRASS KETTLE BURIED BY JESSE JAMES

The next item Joe dug up was a large, old, brass kettle in the Wichita Mountains. To his surprise, it was empty, but there was a lot of excitement over it because there was a definite connection between it and Jesse James and his gang.

The kettle had a lot of writing inscribed on it, and also the names of 11 people: Jesse and Frank James, Cole Younger, Frank Miller, George Overton, Rub Busse, Charlie Jones, Uncle George Payne, Roy Baxter, Mack Smith, and Bud Dalton. The famous outlaw Dalton brothers from Ensign, Kansas had once ridden with the James gang.

Actually, the kettle had served as a contract on which the members of the James gang had bound themselves to an agreement saying that the treasure belonged to them all, equally.

It was dated: "The 5th day of March 1876, The Year of Our Lord." It did not describe the treasure nor where it was hidden, but it must have referred to the cache of treasure that Joe had found earlier nearby, containing the gold bullion, the jewels, coins and the old watch. Presumably, it was to be dug up later and added to the KGC treasures.

Then later, Joe found an old, three-legged, iron, Dutch oven, and inside of it were the chain and the fob that belonged to the gold watch that he had found earlier. That was important because it proved that it had also been put there by the James gang.

The treasure that Joe had found in Oklahoma is not the only Jesse James or other bandit treasure that has been buried there—there are many more, and there are some I know of that have been found; so I'm sure there are many more waiting to be discovered by someone with a good metal detector—Remember what Joe Hunter had found by just looking around and digging and without a metal detector.

After a few more years of finding nothing, Joe had come to a dead-end, but he believed that buried gold was still around the area someplace. So, he began speaking up, trying to find some one who might have some information that would be helpful. That is when he told the story to the local newspaper in hopes that he might find out some more information.

The results from that story resulted in unimaginable events!

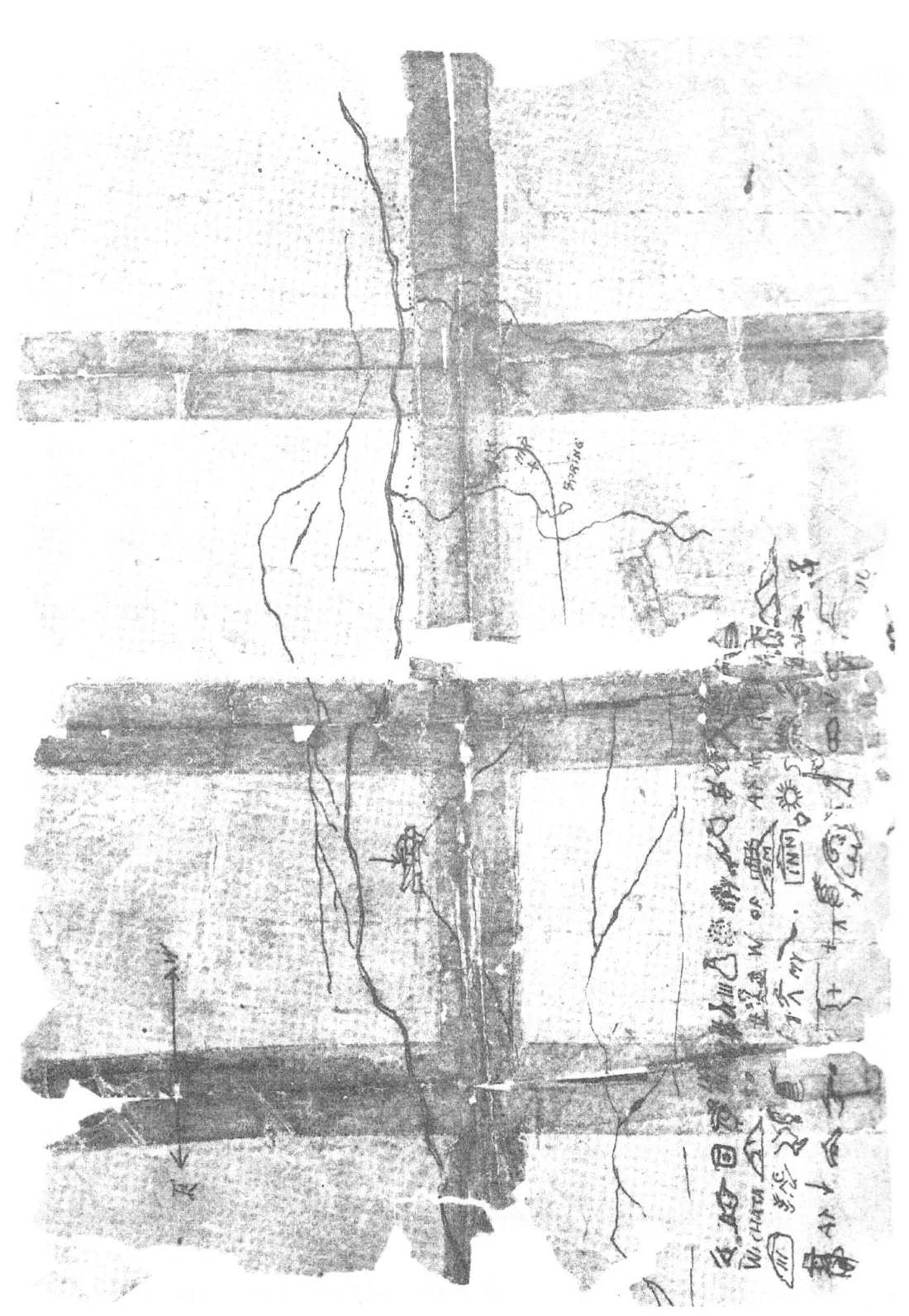

This is one of the old treasure maps that were given to Joe Hunter and his gang had buried some treasure in the Wichita Mountains in Oklahoma. It took years of searching, but Joe finally found it.

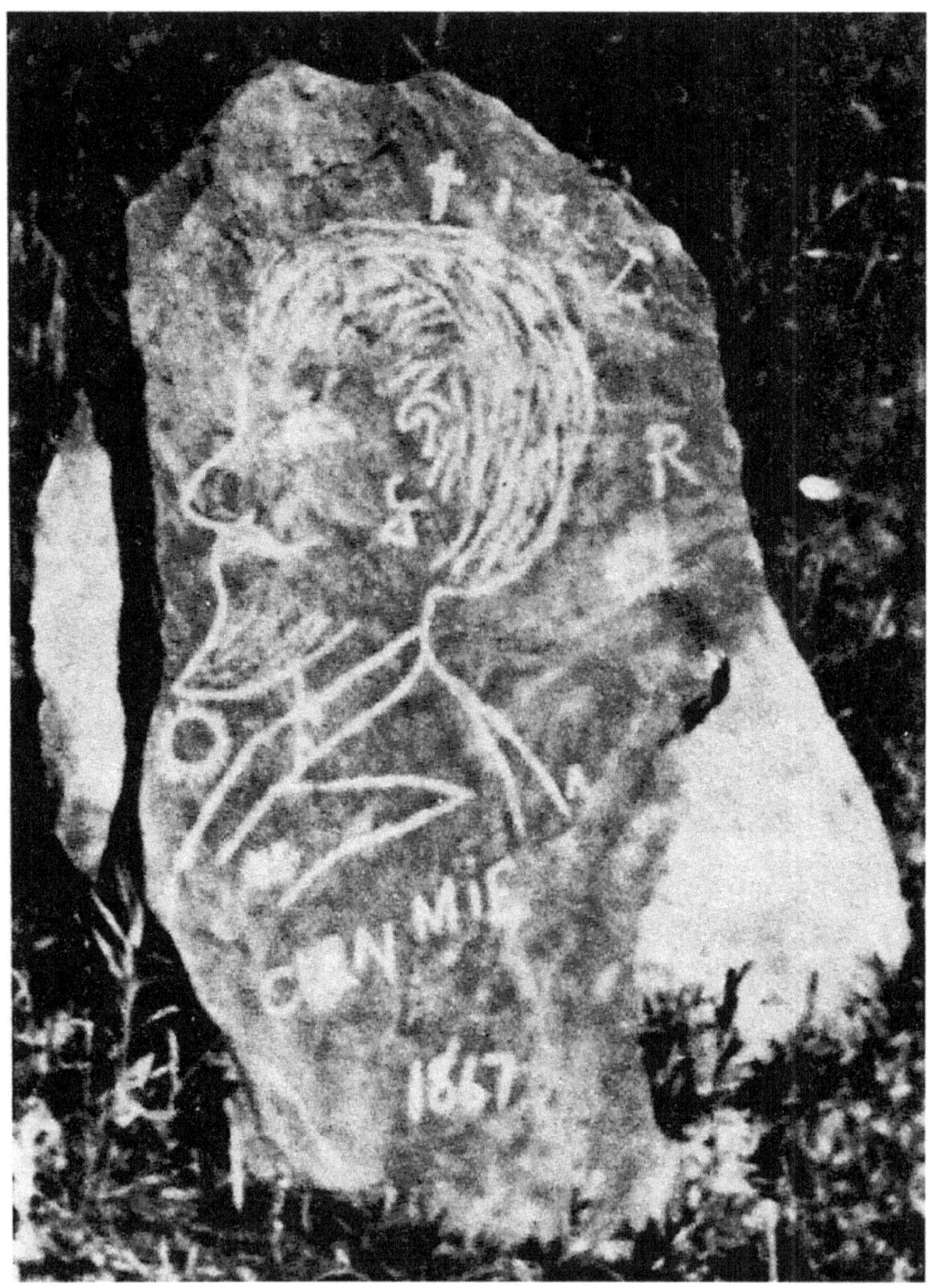

This is the stone map that Frank James had been looking for on Mrs. Belle Hedlund's Ranch after he got out of prison, but he never found it. However, 28 years latter, she discovered it and showed it to Joe Hunter who used it and did find where the treasure was buried.

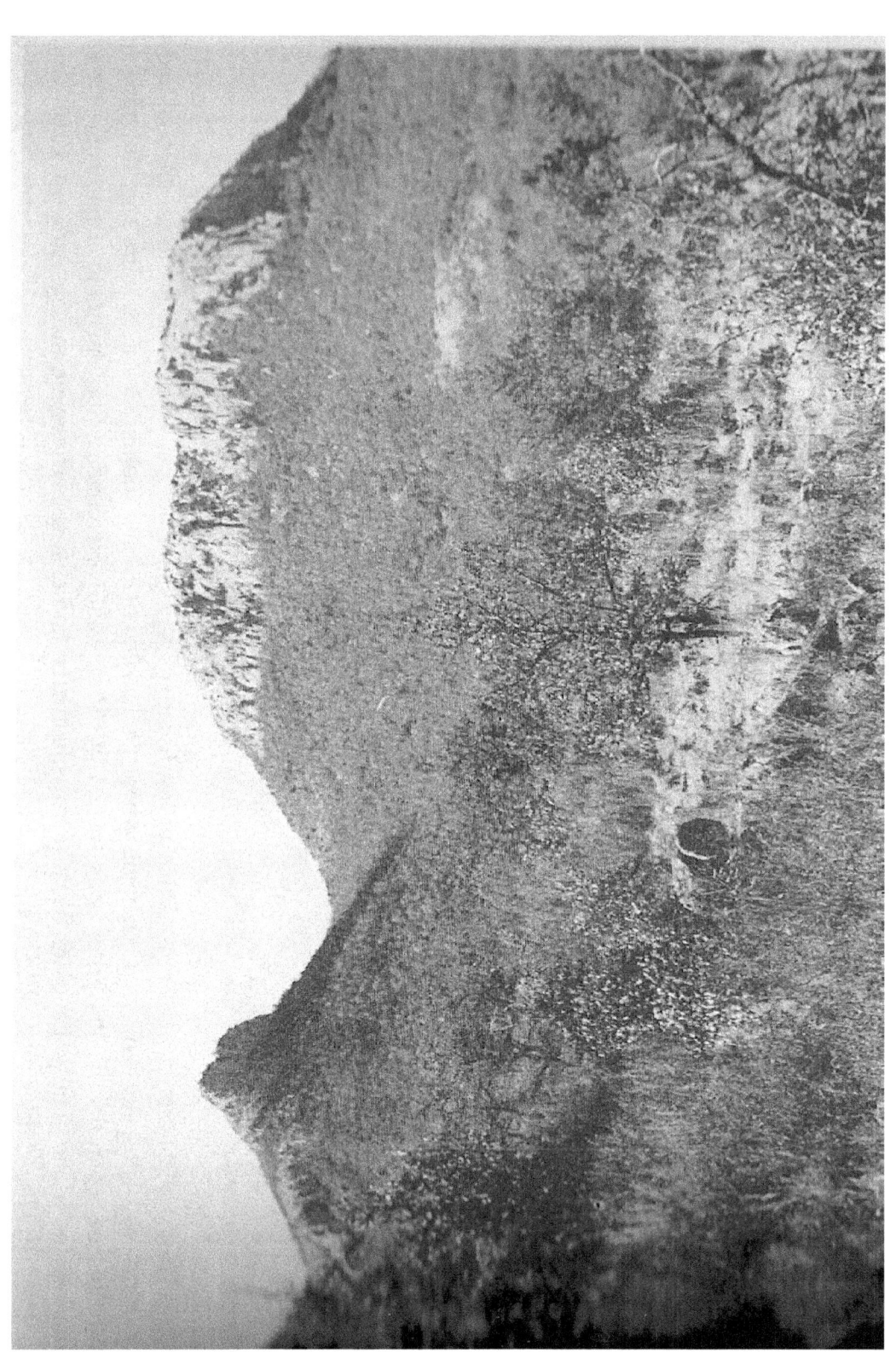

This is a view of the Wichita Mountains in southwestern Oklahoma where Joe Hunter found treasure that had been buried by Jesse James and his gang.

This is the last picture of Frank James at his home in Missouri, before his natural death in 1915 at age of 72. This was after he had left Oklahoma where he had spent years looking for a treasure that the gang had once buried on property that later was owned by Mrs. Belle Hedlund. After spending a number of years looking for it, he finally gave up because the landmarks had changed. However, the treasure was later found in 1937 by Joe Hunter who used some treasure maps to locate it. That was before metal detectors were used.

Chapter Seven

Jesse James Rides Again

Joe Hunter's story in the Lawton Newspaper of finding a Jesse James buried treasure and the brass kettle inscribed with the names of Jesse and Frank James and other members of the gang, plus some strange signs and symbols, attracted wide attention.

It was not long after that when Joe began to receive numerous letters from around the country, especially from one person in Texas who happen to know a little more about secret codes than he did. Then, a few telephone conversations followed.

Several months later, a small cabin plane from Centerville, Texas flew into the Lawton airport. It carried a pilot, two men and a woman. One of the men was very old and had a beard, also a broken hip. They immediately asked for a meeting with Joe Hunter and it was soon arranged.

THE MEETING IN LAWTON

The next morning at the meeting, Joe was told that the name of the old man was J. Frank Dalton. The other man identified himself as Orvus Lee Howk and the woman was his wife, Mary, who was acting as the nurse for the old man.

During the meeting, Joe was absolutely amazed at what he heard from Orvus Lee Howk and the old man. He was also told that Jesse James was still alive. Then Joe heard information from the two men that convinced him that the information they were telling him about some details of the treasure that he had already found, plus others that he was looking for, had to be true.

The next morning, Joe contacted the two main reporters for the Lawton Constitution Newspaper, Lindsey Whitten and Frank Hall, about the surprise meeting he just had during the night, and suggested that they all have a meeting together. The two reporters were the ones who had been writing the stories about Joe Hunter and his search for buried treasure. Both reporters sensed that there could be a lot of good material here for a newspaper story.

They were right--but they had no idea of just how good!

J. FRANK DALTON CLAIMS TO BE JESSE JAMES

The meeting with the two reporters was like a bombshell when Orvus Lee Howk said that right there--the old man in that chair, was the real Jesse James!

Orvus went on to say that Jesse had been living rather quietly down in Texas for a long time, using the assumed name of J. Frank Dalton. The two reporters and Joe Hunter were then shown lots of photographs, newspaper clippings, family letters, etc.

The old man even signed an affidavit that he was the real Jesse Woodson James.

They were all astonished! How could that be true? But before the day was over, the old man and Orvus had pretty much convinced Joe and the two reporters that it was the truth.

However, the two reporters decided that for obvious reasons, they could not publish the story just yet because who would believe that Jesse James was still alive and there in Lawton, Oklahoma at the ripe old age of 100.

They didn't want to be the laughing stock of the world. They needed more time to get more facts and to decide what to do about it. One of the reporters, Hall, had been a native of Missouri, and remembered that as a small child, he had consistently heard rumors that Jesse James was alive, and had not actually been killed as reported.

THE TREASURE AND THEIR SIGNS EXPLAINED

In the meantime, Joe heard more information from the old man about the treasures that he had found, what the signs meant, and how they were buried. He was told an amazing story about how the gang had once discovered some treasure signs in the Wichita Mountains that led them to some gold bars that had been buried by some Mexican miners.

The old man told Joe how they had dug up the gold and reburied it someplace else, leaving some of their own signs around so they could come back for it later. That treasure was apparently what Frank James had been looking for on the woman's farm in Oklahoma after he got out of prison.

The old man said that after they had buried the gold, they decided that since it belonged equally to all of them, they should write out an agreement, but since they had no paper, Jesse said that he then used the old copper kettle to inscribe the agreement on, then buried the kettle himself--empty; and that was the kettle that Joe had found.

There was a photograph taken by the newspaper of Joe and the old man holding the kettle. There was also a copy of the words on the kettle that also gave the date as Fifth of March 1876.

During the next few months, while Whitten and Hall and the newspaper were trying to make up their minds about whether or not they should print the sensational story, Dalton moved into a small tourist cabin. He was not yet sure weather he wanted it announced to the world that he was really Jesse Woodson James, the old notorious outlaw.

After all, he could still maybe face criminal charges, or be in danger of a revenge killing. That was one reason that wherever he went, he always had a loaded six-shooter within an arms reach, and on at least one occasion he demonstrated his ability with it.

WAS HE JESSE JAMES—OR NOT

Meantime, a number of people from around the country who said that they had once known Jesse and could prove whether or not he was still alive, came to see for themselves and to talk to the old man.

It was said that most of them agreed that it was really him--the real Jesse James; especially when they saw his steel blue eyes and the unsmiling face. In most cases, it was said that the old man revealed much information that only the real Jesse James could have known.

Reportable, none of them said that he was not Jesse. However, there were some people who didn't know what to think.

Also, there were features on the old man's body that would match up with the rough and hectic life that he would have lived if he really was Jesse James. He had about 32 scars from bullet wounds, rope burns around his neck from an attempted hanging, the fingernail of one finger was missing, he had some burn scars around his feet, and he appeared to be about 100- years-old. It was obvious that his body bore the signs of a hard, even dangerous, life such as Jesse James would have gone through.

One known incident that would account for the rope burns around his neck happened when Jesse was not yet old enough to join the fighting during the early part of the Civil War; but his older brother, Frank, was fighting with

Quantrills' Raiders. One day, some Union Soldiers came to his house, tied a rope around his neck and hauled him off his feet several times in an effort to make him tell where his brother was. But Jesse wouldn't tell them. A similar incident happened again when some Union Soldiers put his feet into a fire to make him tell where Frank was hiding.

However, some people thought that there were two items that did not match up. Some reports had claimed that Jesse had been shot twice through both lungs during the Civil War that had almost killed him. But some biographies of him don't mention that at all, and Dalton apparently had no matching scars there, Also, the tip of one finger on Jesse was supposedly missing, shot off accidentally as a kid when he dropped a pistol. Dalton only had a missing finger nail on that finger.

Actually, I wonder about the authenticity of the reports that Jesse had been shot twice, through both lungs because I don't see how anyone back then could have survived after being shot like that and still live. Most of the bullets used by the military then were about .50 caliber (one-half-inch in diameter.) That is really a very large and heavy bullet. Perhaps today with our modern medical procedures, we could save a person with wounds that serious…but back then?

As most anyone knows who reads much about Jesse, there are many controversially and conflicting versions of events—and even stories of events that didn't happen at all!

For example: some stories claim that Jesse stood on a chair to dust off a picture frame when Bob Ford shot him, while others claim that he was straightening-up a picture. It was said that Bob Ford had used a .44 caliber gun, but others say it was a .45. But when the body that was exhumed in 1995 from the grave where Jesse was supposedly buried, a .38 caliber bullet was actually found in the head.

It has also been printed that Bob actually killed Charlie Bigelow and not Jesse. Even the stories of the treasure that the gang had buried in Oklahoma that Joe Hunter had found has two widely different versions. The most common one is that they robbed and killed some Mexicans in Mexico who were members of a pack train carrying the treasure; but apparently, the gang actually found it in Oklahoma. I have never read elsewhere that the gang was ever in Mexico. So, maybe the story that Jesse had been shot through the lungs, as some reports claim, didn't happen. We may never know for sure.

Though the bullet wounds and the scars on J. Frank Dalton may sound a bit excessive, Cole Younger, who often rode with the James gang, had 11 new bullets in his body when he was captured after the famous Northfield, Minnesota bank robbery attempt by Jesse and his gang. Then. as he rode in a wagon that was taking him to jail, Cole got up to his feet and bowed to the ladies as the wagon went by.

But when he got out jail later, he went back to his old ways for a while and lived until he was 72-years-old. When he finally died, he had an unbelievable total of 17 bullet wounds in his body, with some of the bullets still there— Apparently, some men in those days were really very tough.

As an interesting note, after Cole Younger got out of prison the last time, he went on a speaking tour around the country on the subject of "What Life Has Taught Me." My father once told me that he had seen Cole Younger in Alva, Oklahoma as he came through to give his talk. That was a number of years before I was born there.

Meanwhile, back in Lawton, the old man was busy and very effectively explaining many questions about his past. Eventually, the newspaper decided that if they were really going to print the story, they would have to do it soon, because rumors were beginning to spread around and other newspapers were beginning to get inquisitive.

HEAD LINES – JESSE JAMES IS ALIVE IN LAWTON

So, on Wednesday, May 19, 1948 the headlines read: "Jesse James is alive In Lawton."

The surprising story went on to say that he was 100-years-old, and was now living in Lawton, Oklahoma. There was also a large photo of him on the front page of the paper that did seem to have the features of what Jesse would look like at that age.

It was sensational!

Within a matter of days, it was like a circus on the streets of Lawton as over 30,000 people, plus other journalist and newsreel photographers from around the world, thronged in to see and hear for themselves when Jesse made his first public appearance.

At that time in 1948, I was attending my second year of college at Oklahoma State University (then known as Oklahoma A&M) in Stillwater, Oklahoma, several hundred miles away. I remember the event well, but among other things, I was too busy with finals to even think about going. Besides, not everybody believed that he was really the true Jesse James. It was an unbelievable story.

HE SAID THAT BOB FORD DID NOT KILL HIM

The old man claimed that Bob Ford had really killed Charlie Bigelow, and that he had never posed as Mr. Howard, and that name was actually the alias for Bob Ford. Also, that he (Jesse) had been using the alias of Jim Crow at the time.

"History was wrong about that," claimed the old man.

He also claimed that he was in the barn when he heard the shot being fired and then went into the house, knowing that his plan had worked.

That story could have certainly been possible since nobody but his family, or some members of his gang, really knew what he looked like at the time. The same went for Charlie Bigelow. Few, if any, would have recognized what Charlie would have looked like…but then, maybe there was no such real person as Charlie Bigelow? Maybe it was a made-up name for whoever it was that got killed? That is a very interesting question, and I wonder if there are any other records anywhere of a Charlie Bigelow, and where did he come from?

Then after the funeral, the old man said that he left the country and went to Brazil and numerous other countries where he lived lawfully for many years under various assumed names. Then eventually, he came back into the United States and went into legitimate business.

Much of what he said coincides with the information that was in the article by Waggoner Carr in Chapter Five, but differs in other ways. However, I'm sure that we will never know all of the facts for certain, and nobody is alive now to confirm or deny most of the information.

Unfortunately, when stories are told and retold, they get further from the truth as time goes on. Also, keep in mind that some of the things he said to people who were listening and to the newspaper reporters, were in some cases not exactly what he might have said.

Sensationalism was alive and well then, just as it is now. And if a small town newspaper had an opportunity to make world headlines with something shocking and contrary to history, it would have been an opportunity too good to pass up, especially if it is embellished a bit.

He apparently told stories of many adventures and of different lives that he had lived—many of them as a soldier and fighter in numerous wars and skirmishes around the world.

The old man intrigued the newspaper reporters and a few others with many stories of his past and possibly cleared up, or filled in, much information that was not generally known. For instance (providing he was as who he claimed to be) that Quantrill's real name was Charles Hart, and that he had graduated from a military school in 1860. He also had a brother by the name of Nat Hart. Why would he have said that if there wasn't some basis for it?

Obviously, one man could not have done all of the things and adventures that he was reported to have said, or maybe he was just trying to impress those who were listening. He was rather talkative at times and enjoyed an audience to which he apparently embellished his stories some—or maybe a lot. However, that does not prove that he was not the real Jesse James.

BELLE STARR

Another story that he told of interest, with a certain amount of softness in his voice, was about Belle Starr, who had been known as the "Bandit Queen." He said that he remembered her as Myra Belle Shirley, daughter of Judge Shirley, of Missouri. She had been a school teacher, but had an adventurous spirit, which had lead her to serve as a spy for the South--- presumably as a KGC member?

He said was that he was shot in the left leg during a skirmish in 1863 in Warsaw, Missouri, but managed to get on a horse and ride away to a school house where he lost conscious from loss of blood. Then, when be awoke, he was lying on a soft bed filled with sunlight and looked up into the face of Myra Belle Shirley who nursed him back to health. For years afterwards, he said, a close friendship existed until she was killed on her 43rd birthday.

Not much has been reported about their association, except she once said that she didn't think the person buried in Missouri was really Jesse James.

The old man was reluctant to discuss details about some of his activities, especially of incidents where people were killed, because of the possibility that capital punishment still existed, even though there wasn't much chance of any witness still being alive then, or located.

One thing that he did talk about and apparently gave accurate background information on was regarding the treasure that Joe Hunter had found and information about what the treasure signs had meant.

JESSE GOES ON A SPEAKING TOUR

There was such a clamor over the sensational news that rather quickly, the old man was getting offers of $100 dollars-a-day, or more, for public appearances, so it wasn't long before the little cabin plane was taking off for Colorado and other places.

He succeeded in going around to a number of states for a couple of years on a speaking tour, in spite of his old age and infirmities, but always accompanied by Orvis Lee Howk and his wife.

HE DIES IN TEXAS IN 1951 AT 104 YEARS OF AGE

Eventually, stories about the old man became old news, and a few years later, he was living back in Texas at Galveston Island, under the care of his "Grandson," it said. But to get relief from the heat and humidity, he was taken to Granbury where he died of pneumonia 10 days later on August 15, 1951 at the given age of 104, and was buried there.

His death certificate is on file in the Hood County Courthouse in Granbury. His grave and tombstone are in the Granbury cemetery. The name on the tombstone is "Jesse Woodson James" and at the bottom is inscribed, "Supposedly Killed in 1882.

But there is another interesting twist at the end of the story. Apparently, the body was exhumed in June 1951 for DNA testing to prove that J. Frank Dalton was really the famous outlaw. That was at the request of some people who claimed that they were the real descendents of Jesse James--but also from numerous other people who believed that Dalton had pulled off one of the greatest hoaxes in history. Apparently, the ones then claiming to be the descendents of Dalton were not the same ones claiming to be the descendents of the body that was buried in Missouri in 1882.

I never found out if there was any DNA tests made, or not--or if there were, maybe it also was inconclusive and not made public? However, one story that I heard was that the wrong body was dug up. It was like 'Déjà vu' again!

But, what could that have proven one way or the other? If the results of the DNA from the old grave in Missouri that was exhumed in 1995, didn't necessarily prove that certain people were, or were not, living relatives of who ever was buried there, the same could hold true for J. Frank Dalton, alias Jesse James, that is buried in Granbury, Texas. And if that DNA did happen to match some people, would that positively prove that they were descendants of the original famous outlaw, Jesse Woodson James; or of someone who just claimed that he was?

Then, to muddy up the water a little bit, as they say, consider how many

Jesse James's were living back then—a lot more than just one or two. In fact, there were quite a few around the country, and that has no doubt led to a number of people today who actually are related to a 'Jesse James'---but which one? I doubt if it will ever be resolved to everybody's satisfaction.

Perhaps the old man's name was really J. Frank Dalton all the time, and was never Jesse James? However, that would be rather hard to investigate and to prove at this time, even if someone could find his name in some old records or censes rolls, and if that name could be found, I doubt if there would be any back-up records to prove his real identify. One problem is that census rolls often used the names of aliases rather than a person's real name.

ORVUS LEE HOWK OR JESSE JAMES III

A few years after J. Frank Dalton had died, Orvus Lee Howk, the man who had brought the old man to Lawton in 1948, decided, for some reason, to tell people that he was Jesse James III, the Great Grandson of Jesse James.

Of course, that was a few years after he had left Oklahoma and Texas for other parts of the country. He had been widely known back there as Orvus Lee Howk, and there had been photos in the newspapers of him and J. Frank Dalton together, and each identified by name.

I happened to be introduced to him here in Hemet, California, a small town near Los Angeles, in 1973 by Del Schrader, the newspaper reporter and author of the well-known book, *"Jesse James Was One of His Names."*

At the time, Del and I were collaborating on information and stories about the KGC and their treasures.

Orvus told us that his name was Jesse James III. At that time, I didn't connect him to the event in Lawton; however, I had a hard time believing that he was really the great grandson of Jesse James.

But that didn't matter much to me at the time because I was an active treasure hunter and Del told me that the man had good information about a treasure chest full of gold coins that was buried at Glorieta Pass in New Mexico by the KGC.

After a few more meetings with the man, he gave Del and I the information we needed to go look for the treasure, which we did.

He said that he had never been there but had been given the information by his great grandfather, Jesse James. I still did not know that he was referring to the old man in Lawton, or that his real name was Orvus Lee Howk.

But Del and I noticed that he did not ask us for money ahead of time. That was most unusual and rather convincing to us since everyone I had know before who said they had information on treasures, always wanted money ahead of time for the information. He did not. He only wanted one- third of whatever we found.

Sure enough, when Del and I got to Glorieta Pass, the signs that he told us to look for were there. And a few hours later, I was able to figure out the signs and started digging at the very edge of a big dry wash, but then discovered that the treasure chest had just recently been washed out by a big spring flood that had undercut the side of the wash; and it had been found by some one who had lived nearby. However, we could still plainly see the outline of where the chest had been, and also some old pieces of the chest, but no treasure. We found out later that the person had moved to Albuquerque and was spending a lot of money.

Later, Orvis told Del and I about numerous other KGC treasures, but none of them close enough for either of us to go look for. Besides, I had learned by that time what his real name was, and I had lost some confidence in what he was saying.

Even though I didn't believe by then that he was related to any of the James family, I kept wondering how he seemed to have all of this information about treasures and other events in history, and some of it proved accurate? In fact, I could not prove that any of it was false, though some of it was rather suspicious.

He always seemed to have a quick answer, or explanation, for about anything. Both Del and I agreed that he was a brilliant man. Then after I found out what his real name was, I concluded that he had decided to take advantage of his information on the KGC and Jesse James' treasures, and it would be more effective if he claimed to be related to Jesse James.

Perhaps, something like that is what he had in mind years before when he brought the old man up from Texas in 1948 to announce to the world that Jesse James was still alive. Orvos knew a good opportunity when he saw it— whether he thought the old man was the real Jesse James, or not, and knew that as the promoter of a man who claimed to be the real Jesse James, it could put money in his pocket. Also, Orvus obviously enjoyed a lot of special attention.

One thing that can be said for sure about Orvus was that he was a good opportunist, had a very quick mind, and always had a good answer for everything —whether it happened to be true, or not…and in some cases, I found that it really was true!

SOME INTERESTING QUESTIONS

If the old man in Lawton wasn't who he said he was, then how did he know the information and background of the treasure that Joe Hunter had been looking for and eventually found in the Wichita Mountains in Oklahoma?

And if he wasn't who he said he was, then how did his friend, Orvus Lee Howk, know many details of the KGC treasure at Glorieta Pass in New Mexico that I found to be accurate when I went there and found the signs he described and where the treasure chest had been, though Orvus told me that he himself had never been there.

Then according to a newspaper article that I have, Orvus and a partner recovered a treasure of 14 gold bars worth $600.000 in New Mexico in 1962 that supposedly had been hidden by Jesse James as part of the KGC treasure. Also, he apparently had located a safe full of money in the bottom of the Brazos River in Waco, Texas, but when the safe was pulled to the surface of the river, it slipped and plunged back to the bottom of the river and could not be located again.

Orvus also had a lot of information about the KGC and of their treasures that were buried or hidden around the country. Apparently, he had boxes full of this information that contained newspaper articles, letters, maps, photographs, etc. I saw some of these items that he showed me here in California…most of which was revealed in my book a few years ago: *"The Mysterious and Secret Order of The Knights of The Golden Circle."*

FRANK 'PISTOL PETE' EATON

Orvus told me a lot about various historical events and about some other famous men, that in some cases I happened to know were correct. One of those was about the famous old gunfighter, Frank 'Pistol Pete' Eaton who lived in Enid, Oklahoma where I attended High School there in 1938. He was famous and his story is told in the book: *"Pistol Pete, Frank Eaton"* published by Signet Books in 1958.

Frank Eaton, as a kid at eight-years-old in Eastern Kansas, had seen his parents and his younger sister being brutally killed by a gang of six outlaws in 1868. The next day, he started learning to shoot. He swore that he would become a gun expert and hunt them down and kill them all—which he did. He took lessons from some of the most famous gunmen in our history,

He became perhaps the fastest draw of all time. He also became an Indian fighter, an Army Scout, and a gun-hand for the Cattlemen's Association. I had met him a few times and had watched him put on several fancy shooting demonstrations, including his famous 'fast draw' at the annual Cherokee Strip Celebration in Enid.

The feature movie *"Nevada Smith"* starring Steve McQueen was based on his life. I was quite privileged to have seen, up close and personal on several occasions this living legend of the Real Old Wild West.

He also looked every bit the character that he was, and its quite possible that he had known, or associated with the real Jesse James, and/or Frank Dalton at one time.

Frank always wore high cowboy boots with spurs, a cowboy hat, carried a loaded .45 Colt Revolver, had a large mustache, and had his hair in braids. To my knowledge, he never owned a car, but always rode his buck-skin horse into town and tied the horse up to a parking meter and never put any money into it. If the cops showed up, they pretended not to notice the overdue meter sign, but would introduce themselves and get into an interesting conversation with him. After all, they knew how fast he was on the draw, and decided not to provoke a real gunfighter with a loaded .45 in his open holster, even though there was a city ordnance against carrying a loaded gun in town, and using a parking meter space with out putting money into it. There is a photograph of him on page 69 in my first book: *"The Mysterious and Secret Order of the Knights of The Golden Circle."*

So, if the old man in Lawton was not who he claimed to be, then how was he able to supply so much information and so many details about Jesse James and what he did; and if his friend, Orvus Lee Howk, didn't get the information that he was telling about Jesse James and of the KGC treasure sites from him, then where did it come from?

DID JESSE EVER USE THE NAME OF DALTON

There seems to be some evidence that J. Frank Dalton and Jesse James were the same person. According to one researcher who made a very thorough search of many old records, he found that Jesse had started using aliases back during the time of the Civil War when he and his brother were being sought by Union Soldiers, then later by the Pinkertons; and "Dalton" was one of them. We know that Jesse had used a number of different alias's, at different times, and he had been using the alias of "Mr. Howard" when Bob Ford supposedly shot him.

CONCLUSION

Was Jesse James really a member of The KGC? We really don't know for sure, but there is much information, plus some logic, that he was.

In fact, when the gang derailed and robbed the Rock Island Train at Adair, Iowa on June 21, 1873, they all wore Ku Klux Klan masks; and there could have been other occasions when they did it again. The Ku Klux Klan was the military arm of the KGC.

Since the KGC was a very secret society that went underground after the Civil War, its membership was not public knowledge, so it's hard to know who was a member and who was not.

Was there really a secret organization called "The Knights of The Golden Circle" or the KGC? Indeed there really was (and maybe still is.) Only a part of their whole story is known today, but some of their activities are still a matter of public records.

Did the KGC secretly bury a vast amount of treasure around the United States? Yes, there is no doubt about it. In fact, I have seen physical evidence of it and have examined some of their sites.

Did Jesse James bury some of the treasures for the KGC? Again, we really don't know for sure, but there are some good indications that he did. Also, there is photographic evidence taken of the old brass kettle found by Joe Hunter in Oklahoma showing Jesses' and Franks' names, plus some others in his gang that referred to a sizable treasure they had just buried with plans to come back for it later. Otherwise, why wouldn't they have taken the treasure with them and not buried it?

Did Bob Ford really kill Jesse James, or was it someone else that got killed; and was the whole thing a hoax? Again, we really don't know for sure, but there seems to be enough convincing evidence that it was all a hoax.

Was Orvus Lee Howk, who later claimed that he (himself) was Jesse James III, really the great grandson of the real Jesse James, or of J. Frank Dalton?

No, I'm sure that he was not blood-related to either, but he had known J. Frank Dalton rather well; and it was apparently from him that he learned a lot about some hidden treasures. But were these KGC treasures, Jesse James treasures, or treasures buried by someone else? That really is puzzling, and I will probably never find out for sure

Was J. Frank Dalton really the famous old outlaw, Jesse James? Again, we really don't know for sure, but there seems to be a lot of evidence that he really was.

WHATS IN A NAME

At this point of this book, I got to thinking a lot about the name that the old man had been using for his alias. I have always felt that there was something of substance behind the name of "J. Frank Dalton." Somehow, there seemed to be some kind of a connection between it and the real Jesse James. I had always been suspicious of it, especially since he only used an initial for the first name. What was the reason for that? It was rather strange. Not many people use only an initial for their first name.

Yes—maybe that was what was bothering me the most! But also, using the last name of Dalton seemed a bit too strange, or too much of a

coincidence. Why would he use that name since the Dalton gang were well known bank robbers at the time. It really got me to wondering!

Obviously, the reason he used an initial to start his alias name with would have been a give-away as to who he really was. Apparently, no one ever asked him what the "J" stood for, or if they did, he probably ignored it.

But, think about it!

Of course!--The "J" stands for "Jesse," "Frank," for his brother, and "Dalton" from his mother's maiden name since she was born a member of that family. So, he put them all together and used it for an alias.

How clever!

I suppose that by using that alias, he felt a little more comfortable with it since it wasn't a complete separation from who he really was, but it was disguised enough for him to hide behind, and it's all the more reason to believe that the old man was really Jesse James!

The legend of Jesse James and of the KGC will live on for generations and will always be a matter of great interest to historians and to the general public.

It's possibly that someday there will be enough convincing evidence on these subjects that it may rewrite some of our history.

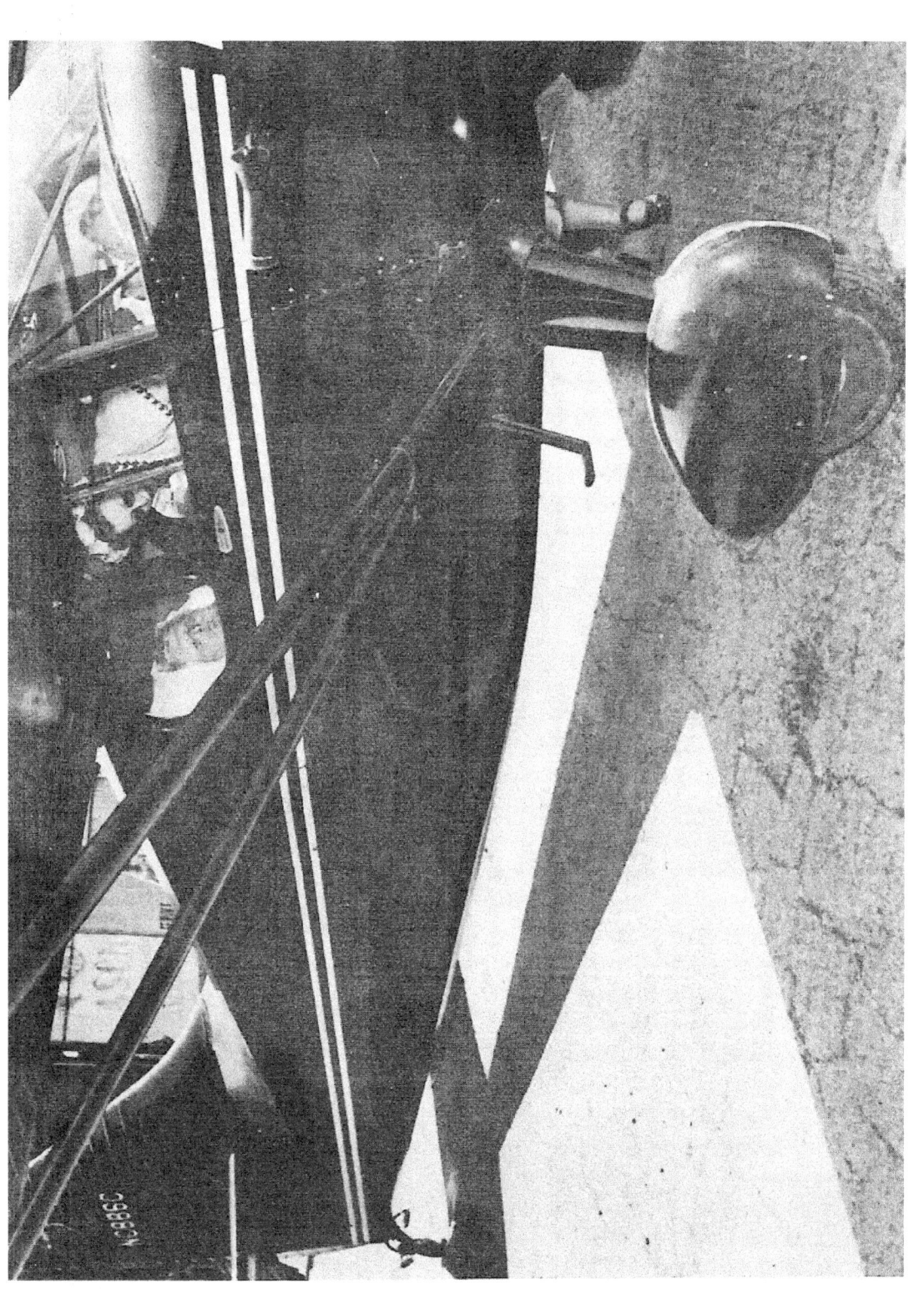

Here is the small cabin plane that brought Jesse in to Lawton from Texas in 1948, and also the plane that left Lawton several months later to take Jesse on a speaking tour to a number of states. Jesse is seen in the back and the woman in front was identified as his nurse, Mrs. Orvus Lee Howk. When I met Orvus and his wife, Mary, here in Los Angeles in 1973, Orvus told me that his name was Jesse James III, the great grandson of Jesse James, though I really didn't believe him.

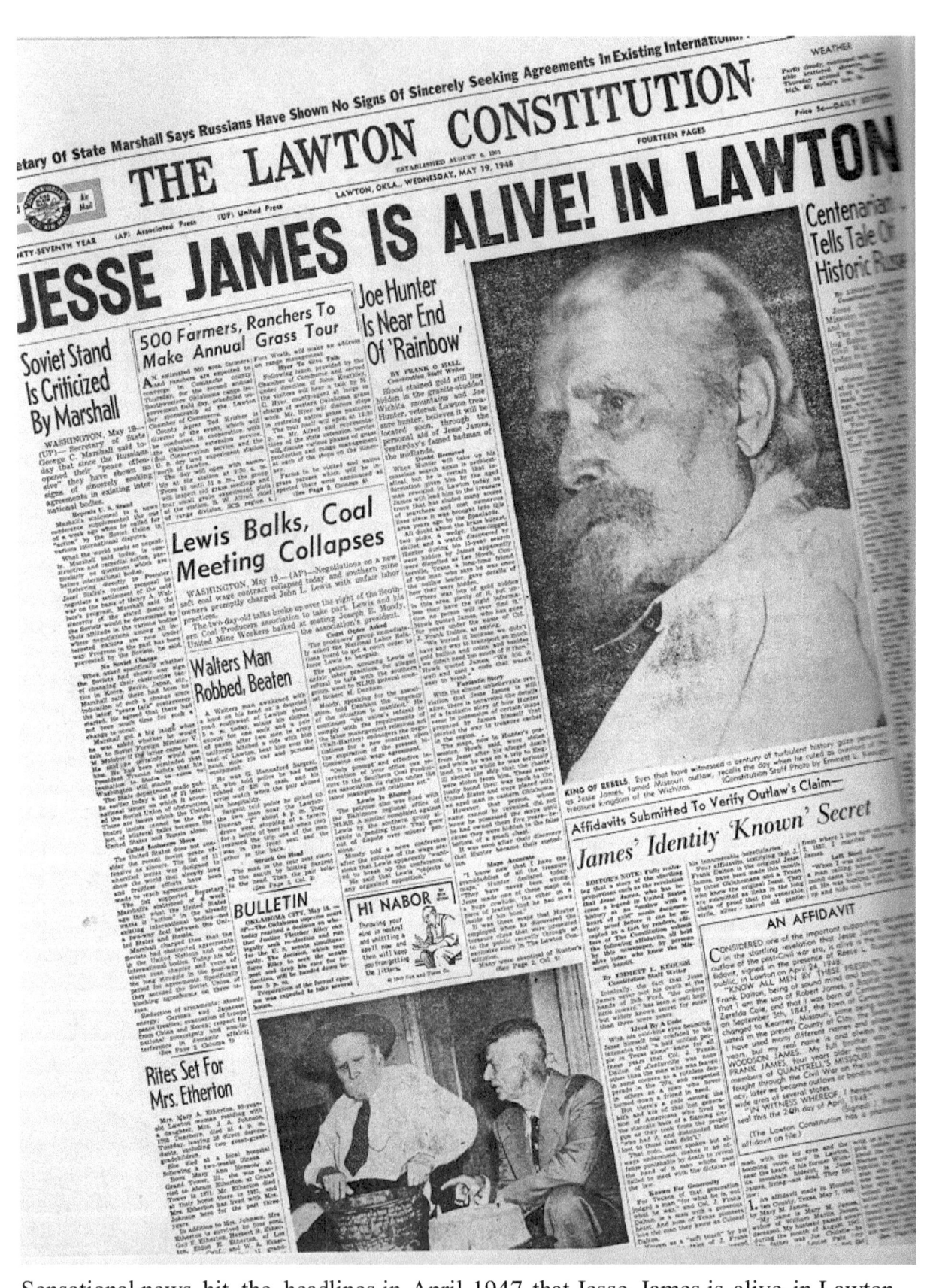

Sensational news hit the headlines in April 1947 that Jesse James is alive in Lawton, Oklahoma at the ripe old age of 100.

In a few days after the surprising headlines in April 1948, a crowd of about 20,000 people thronged in to Lawton, Oklahoma to see for themselves the old man who said that he was the real Jesse James that had supposedly been killed by Bob Ford in 1882.

An Affidavit

Considered one of the most important supporting documents in the startling revelation that Jesse James, legendary outlaw of the post civil war era is still alive is the following affidavit, signed in the presence of Reece L. Russell, notary public in Lawton On April 24 1948.:

"KNOW ALL MEN BY THESE PRESENTS: That I, J. Frank Dalton, being of sound mind and body, wish to state that I am the son of Robert James, a Baptist minister, and Zerelda Cole, and that I was born at Centerville, Missouri, on September 5th, 1847. The town of Centerville was later changed to Kearney, Missouri, same being located and situated in the present County of Clay, the State of Missouri. I have used many different names and aliases over many years, but my real name is and always has been JESSE WOODSON JAMES. My full brother was ALEXANDER FRANK JAMES, four years older than myself. We were members of QUANTRILL'S MISSOURI IRREGULARS that fought through the Civil War on the side of the Confederacy, later we became outlaws or bandits who operated over a wide area of several states.

"IN WITNESS WHEREOF, I hereunto set my hand and seal this the 24th day of April, 1948."

(Signed) J. Frank Dalton.

J. Frank Dalton signed this affidavit in April 1948 declaring that he was the real Jesse Woodson James, the old bandit outlaw.

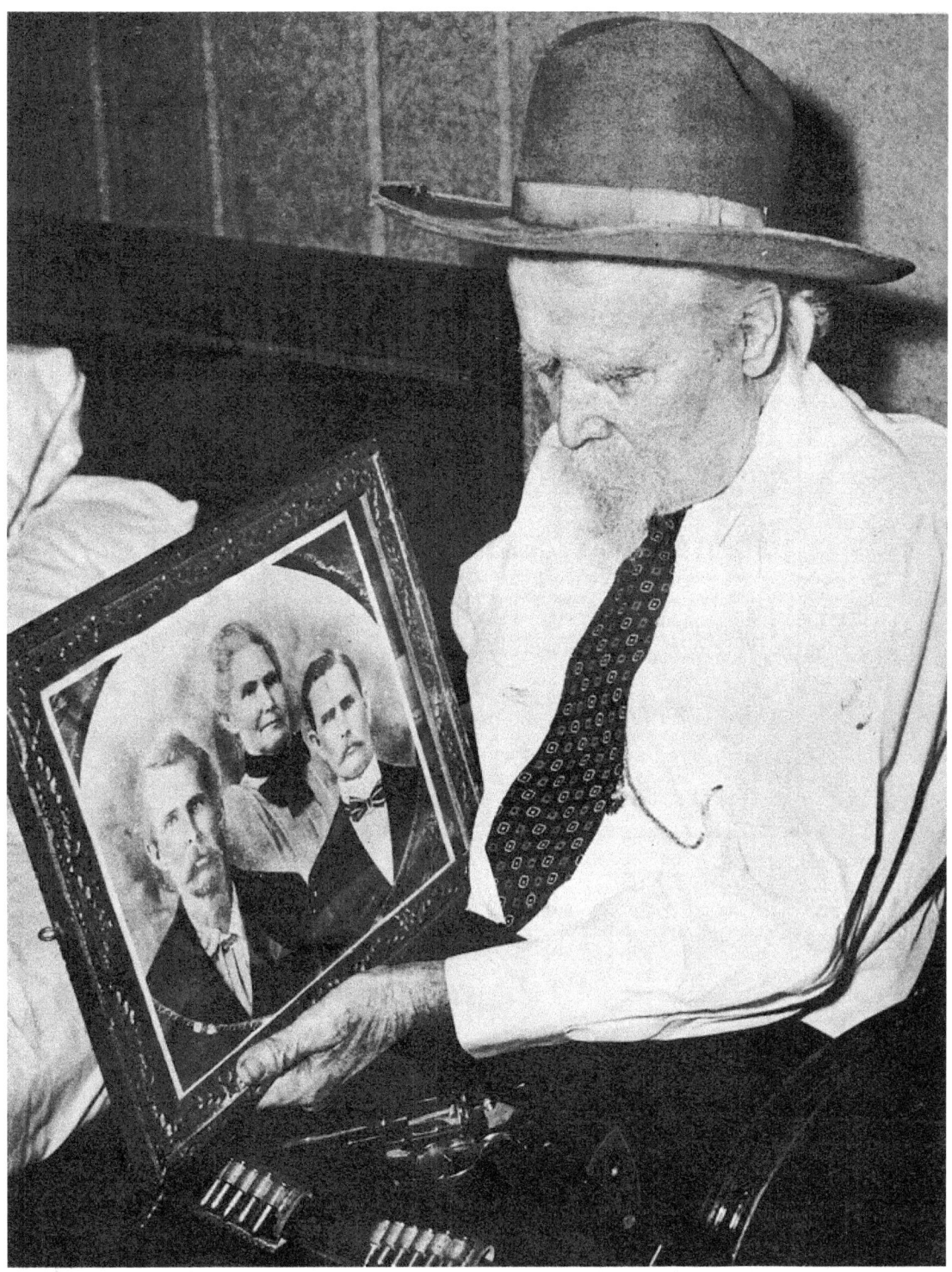

Here is Jesse, looking at an old family portrait of himself shown on the left, his mother in the center and his brother, Frank, on the right. Note the six-shooter on his lap, along with the bullets in his gun belt, that he always kept within easy reach--just in case!

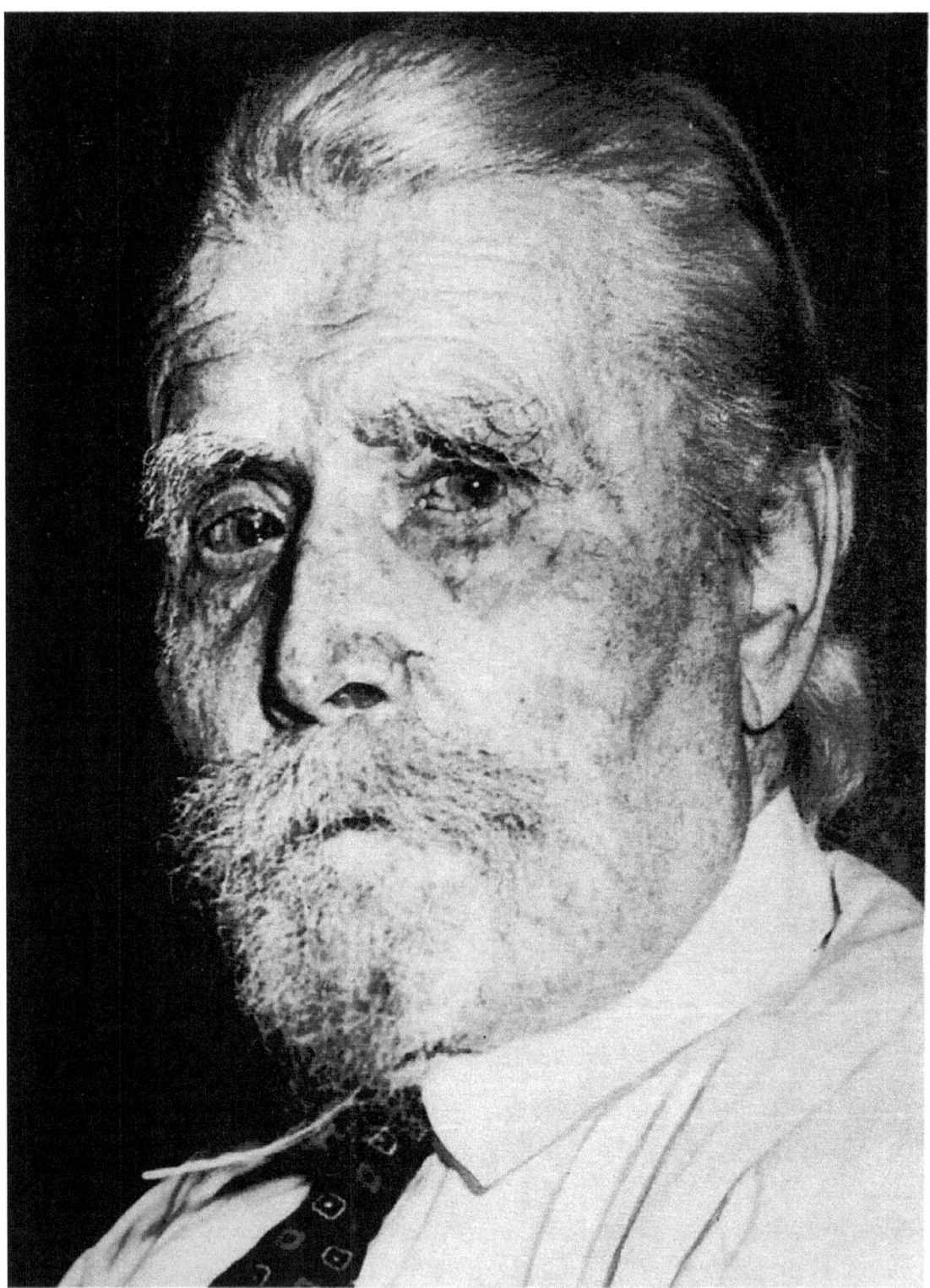
Jesse James (Alias J. Frank Dalton) at 100-years-old. Notice his piercing eyes. That was one of Jesse's noticeable characteristics that helped convince many people that it was really him.

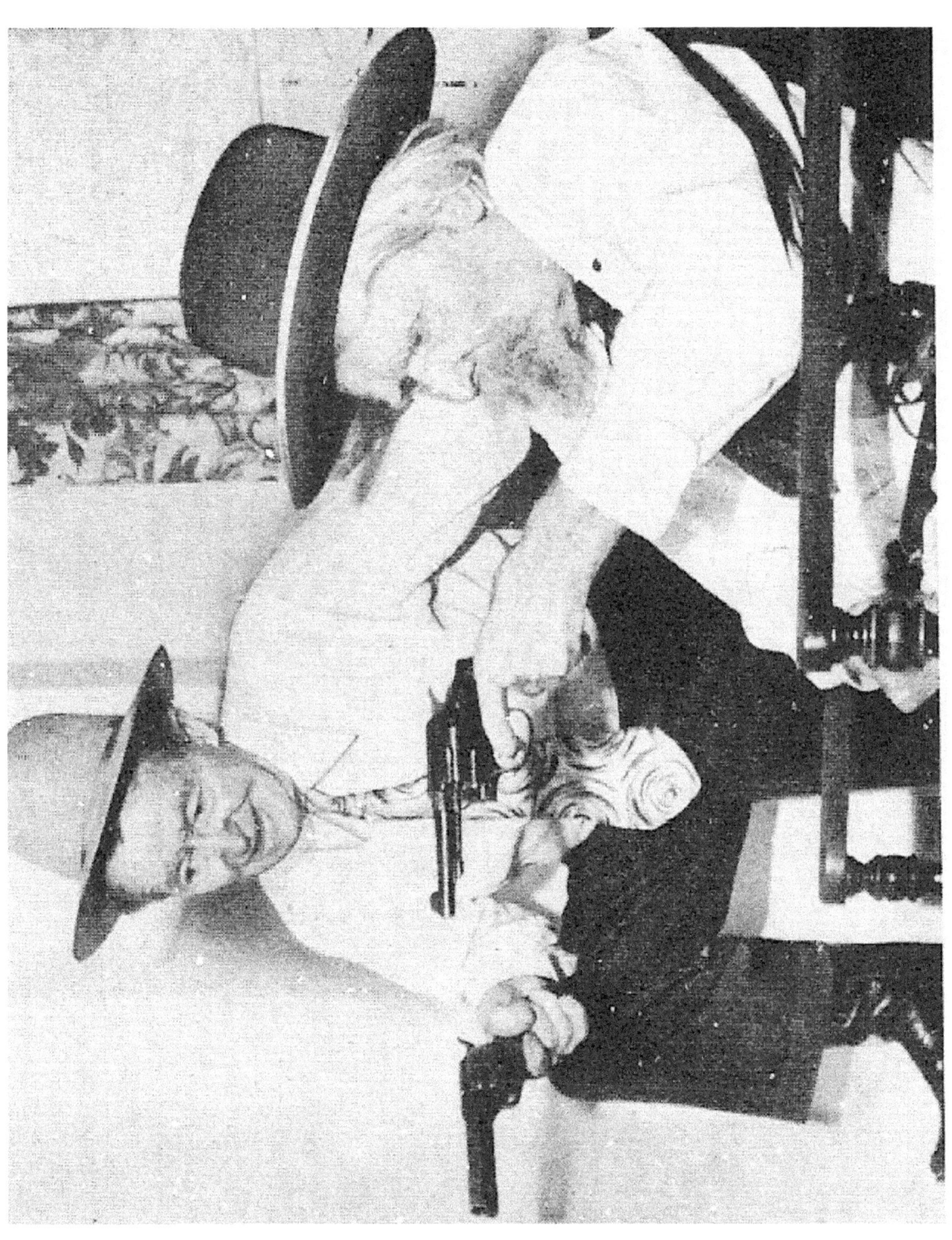

This photo shows Jesse (alias J. Frank Dalton) on the right, with the old famous Oklahoma outlaw and train robber, Al Jennings--both posing with their six-shooters. Al was brought in to identify the old man, and he said, "Boys, there isn't a bit of doubt on earth. It's him. It's Jesse James."

Jesse and Lawton treasure seeker, Joe Hunter, examine the old brass kettle that Jesse and his gang had buried 70 years before in the Wichita Mountains in Oklahoma. Joe had found it by following some old treasure maps. However, it was empty since it had only been used to inscribe a contract on by Jesse to say that the treasure the gang had just buried nearby in the Old Dutch Oven belonged to all of them-- equally. Joe had found the Dutch Oven first with the sizable treasure in it. Then later, found the kettle that referred to it. Also shown are the pick heads that had been left as treasure signs.

This is Jesse taking a close-up look at the old brass kettle that he had inscribed the contract on, plus the names of the gang, after they had buried a sizable treasure nearby in an old, three-legged, Dutch oven.

Orvus Lee Hawk is shown here on the right with Jesse James (alias J. Frank Dalton) and the brass kettle that is setting on top of the old, three-legged, Dutch Oven, along with the pick-heads. It was Orvus who had persuaded Jesse to come out of hiding in Texas and go to Lawton to reveal who he was.

Addendum Section

This is a most important picture of Bob Ford. However, it is usually shown in small size like this one so that the details cannot be noticed. It shows Bob after he had presumably killed Jesse James. He is holding a pearl-handled .45 Colt Revolver that he said he had used. He claimed that it had been a gift from Jesse himself, though some records say that he had used a .44 Smith & Wesson. But, strangely enough, in about 1995, when the body that was exhumed from the grave in Missouri where Jesse James was supposed buried, a .38 caliber bullet was found in the skull—Obviously, something doesn't add up here, and there has always been a big doubt over whether he really killed Jesse, or not, even though history says that he did.

But now, I believe that there is clear evidence to settle that issue, once and for all--and it is in this photograph that shows Bob Ford sending a very subtle but obvious message that he did not kill Jesse James. He has very carefully posed for this picture so that his message can be seen, but maybe not immediately recognized. Look very carefully and consider--isn't it strange that he is holding the gun in his left hand when he was apparently right-handed? Also, why does he have his right foot up on a step so that his right leg is noticeable higher than his left; and why does he have his right leg covered with a very dark cloth and with his right hand above it in a noticeable way--like intentionally to attract attention to it?

Actually, he is doing just that! But since this photo has normally been printed in small format, like this one, or even had parts of it trimmed off, the details have not been noticeable. But turn to the next page to see what had been unnoticed for all these years—and see the rest of the story that should set the record straight!

    This is a very carefully posed photo of Bob Ford in which he is sending a clear, but subtle, message that he did not kill Jesse James. Note the elevated right leg with a dark cover over it to make it more noticeable that he has his 'trigger finger' crossed with another finger. Also, he is holding the gun in his 'left' hand instead of his right, and he has it pointing almost directly to his crossed fingers. How much more obvious could it be?

SPECIAL NOTE ON THE PHOTO TO THE LEFT…WHY DOES BOB FORD HAVE HIS FINGERS CROSSED?
BECAUSE HE DID NOT SHOOT JESSE JAMES!

After I had completed the text for this book and was selecting various photos to include, I found this photo in my collection of Bob Ford. It is the well-known photo of him posing as the killer of Jesse James. It is rarely shown on a full-sized-page in large format like this one, sharp and clear, so that you can see the details of it.

Most of the time when this photo has appeared, it has been reduced down to a much smaller size and is usually a copy made from other copies and the details can not be seen. Also, it often has been trimmed down to only show the center part of the photo—mainly just Bob's face, his body and the revolver, but not extending out to the area of his right hand. However, this is the entire photo as it was taken, and clearly shows the complete picture.

Then, as I took a good look at this one, something attracted my attention, and that was why does his right pants leg appear much darker and larger than his left leg?

I began to wonder if it had resulted from unequal lighting, then decided that it was not. Then on closer observation, I could see that there was a dark cover placed over his right leg. But why? That was very strange. I also thought that he seemed to be holding something under his right hand--but what was it?

So, I enlarged the photo, and to my surprise, I could clearly see that it was his finger.

He had his fingers crossed--one under the other--And one was his trigger-finger!

I was astonished at that!

Also, I noticed that the other two fingers on his right hand were carefully curled back underneath his hand so that only his two crossed-fingers were visible.

It was obviously a very clear, but subtle, hand signal that he did not kill Jesse James! And it has been overlooked for years—until now!

Remember when we were kids that if we said something while we had our fingers crossed, that meant that we had not been telling the truth, or had been telling a lie or something that was not true. It was mostly a kid's game, but sometimes we did it on our parents and got away with it.

Then I realized why he had taken the trouble to put a black cover over his right leg— otherwise, his crossed fingers would not have shown over his light-colored suit. I'm sure that it was not to cover up a hole or worn spot since it's obviously a brand new suit. Otherwise, there is absolutely no reason or advantage of taking the trouble of putting a black cover over his right leg—That was a strange and unnecessary thing to do.

Also, I noticed he was holding the gun in his left hand. Why would he do that when he was right-handed? All of the sketches of him shooting Jesse were shown with him using his right hand. I also noticed that he was pointing the gun in the direction of his two crossed fingers.

I believe that Bob Ford was getting tired of living a lie and his conscience was bothering him. I believe he did not like being thought of as a cowardly assassin, a villain, and being despised by a lot of people, and being the main figure in a hoax of major portion. I think he didn't want to leave a legacy of cowardliness about him in history—which seems to have happened anyway, mostly with the song: *"That Dirty Little Coward That Shot Mr. Howard."*

I think he wanted to somehow set the record straight, but he could not come out directly and say so at the time because that would undo what had been so carefully worked out. So, he left a subtle message that he believed would be understood later.

Otherwise, then explain why the photo was taken from his left side with him holding the gun in his left hand when he was thought to be right-handed. Why wasn't it taken from the right side with him holding the gun in his right hand as would be expected?

That's because he wanted to show the trigger-finger on his right hand, crossed. If he had shown the fingers crossed on his left hand, that would not have been as significant as with his right hand. He obviously wanted things to appear differently than they should have been. So, this pose had been very carefully thought out ahead of time.

Apparently, this is the first time that this very important piece of history has been noticed. But unless some one had enlarged the photo, it would not have been noticed!

I have purposely not gone back to change my text to include this late information, since I had judged and written this book on the basis of information that was available to me at that time. However, this photo does support the theory and information that Bob Ford did not shoot Jesse.

I believe it was another person that was killed and buried in Missouri as some people have always said. Maybe it was Charlie Bigelow, as previously mention, since he was similar in appearance to Jesse. But who ever it was, was probably not killed by Bob Ford.

It was more likely someone who had been killed by Jesse himself. Jesse was known for his hot temper and being quick on the draw. In fact, a short time before, he had just killed someone he didn't like, so perhaps it had happen again; and Jesse could see it as part of a clever plan so that Bob could claim the reward and he (Jesse) could escape from the law. I believe that Bob was a good friend of Jesses' and cooperated with him on this venture.

That also explains why nobody in the gang went after Bob to kill him since they all knew it had been arranged and that Bob had really done Jesse a big favor. That was also believed by numerous other people at the time who always thought that Jesse was still alive.

History Should Be Rewritten!

About the Author, Dr. Roy W. Roush, Ph.D.

The author is one of the most recognized names in the world as an authority on the subject of Treasure Hunting and Gold Prospecting for over 40 years. He has also been very active in those fields and has served as a researcher and consultant for a number of organizations, individuals, and television programs: plus organizing and participating in various treasure expeditions and underwater salvage projects in the Florida Keys, the Bahamas, Turks and Caicos Islands, Mexico, Puerto Rico, and Europe, as well as throughout the United States.

Obtaining a B.A. Degree in Journalism in 1950, he used his journalism expertise to write for many of the treasure hunting publications including: *"Treasure," "Treasure Hunter," "Treasure Search," "Treasure Found," "Treasure News,"* and the *"Treasure Hunter Confidential Newsletter."* Later, he earned a Ph.D. in Archaeology.

During World War II, (at age 17) he fought as a front-line combat rifleman with the US Marine Corps Second Marine Division during the famous battles of Guadalcanal, Tarawa, Saipan, and Tinian in the South Pacific as a Corporal. Then, during the Korean War, he joined the U.S Air Force as a pilot and officer and flew jet fighters and P-51 Mustangs. After discharge, he flew as a Commercial Pilot for a while. Recently, he authored a major book about his experiences in combat and as an Air Force fighter pilot, entitled *"OPEN FIRE."* (Website:) OPEN-FIRE.US

Being one of the first to use a metal detector in the early 1960's (building his first one in 1962), he has searched for many of the well-know lost treasures, including: the Lost Dutchman; the 17 Tons of Mexican Gold in New Mexico; Peg Leg's Black Gold Nuggets; Iron Door Mine; Knights of the Golden Circle Treasures; Vasquez's Bandit Loot; Lost Arch Mine; Black Beard's Treasure; etc.

As an expert with all kinds of metal detectors, he has won numerous National Metal Detecting Contests. His collection of items found is impressive. He has taught courses on Treasure Hunting, Ghost Towns and Gold Prospecting at UCLA, Los Angeles City College, the Elks Lodge in Glendale, Keene Engineering, Treasure Emporium, and has taught Metal Detecting to the FBI. He is the consultant to the Los Angeles City Police Department on Metal Detecting, Currently, he is featured in the popular commercial video *"Prospecting for Gold,"* available at most Gold Prospecting and Treasure Hunting shops on DVD or VHS.

He is a popular guest speaker on these subjects to many clubs and organizations, including "The Gene Autry Museum of Western History;" "The

Gold Prospectors Association," "The Adventures' Club of Los Angeles," and has himself been the subject of many newspaper and magazine articles, television and radio programs. He has served as technical consultant for numerous treasure publications and television programs--plus featured in some, including: *"Unsolved Mysteries," "The Treasure Hunters," "The Search for Amazing Treasures," Bill Burrud's "Treasure Series,"* NBC's specials on "Gold Prospecting" and *"Treasure Hunting." Then recently on History Channels', "Jesse James' Lost Treasure."*

He owns one of the largest private libraries on Treasure Hunting in the world that includes thousands of books, magazine and newspaper articles, videos, tapes and photographs.

www.ingramcontent.com/pod-product-compliance
Lightning Source LLC
Chambersburg PA
CBHW060317240426
43661CB00059B/2790